# CONTENTS

a player's guide to

# chords&harmony

## Music Theory for Real-World Musicians

by Jim Aikin

Backbeat
Books
San Francisco

Published by Backbeat Books
600 Harrison Street, San Francisco, CA 94107
www.backbeatbooks.com
email: books@musicplayer.com

An imprint of CMP Information
Publishers of *Guitar Player, Bass Player, Keyboard,* and *EQ* magazines

CMP
United Business Media

Distributed to the book trade in the US and Canada by
Publishers Group West, 1700 Fourth Street, Berkeley, CA 94710

Distributed to the music trade in the US and Canada by
Hal Leonard Publishing, P.O. Box 13819, Milwaukee, WI 53213

Front cover design by Ren Dolnick
Front cover photos by Getty Images (score: Harnett/Hanzon; keyboard:
     Greg Kuchik; guitar neck: David Toase)
Back cover design by Damien Castaneda

Library of Congress Cataloging-in-Publication Data

Aikin, Jim.
A player's guide to chords & harmony : music theory for real-world musicians /
by Jim Aikin.— 1st ed.
     p. cm.
Includes index.
ISBN 0-87930-798-6 (alk. paper)
1. Harmony. 2. Chords (Music) 3. Musical intervals and scales. I. Title: Player's
guide to chords and harmony. II. Title.

MT50.A37 2004
781.2'5—dc22

                                    2004002014

Printed in the United States of America

04  05  06  07  08    5  4  3  2  1

# PREFACE

When I was a junior in high school, I was fortunate enough to be able to take an entire year of music theory as part of my accredited classwork. Given how checkered my college career was about to become (hey, it was the Sixties, what can I say?), it's extremely fortunate that I was able to get a thorough grounding in harmony theory at such an early date. Not everyone is so lucky.

The text we used in that high-school class was Walter Piston's *Harmony* [Norton]. Now, *Harmony* is a wonderful book. If you're serious about learning music theory, you'd be foolish not to read and study it, or another book like it. At the same time, it has to be admitted that Piston is perhaps not quite right for everyone. He begins by explaining, in detail, how to write four-part chorales in the style of Bach — not a skill that most musicians need on a regular basis. And there's not a word in his book on jazz chords or how to read chord charts. All of his examples are drawn from classical music, and most of them from pre-20th-century classical music.

More recently, I've been looking at a textbook called *Harmony & Voice Leading*, by Edward Aldwell and Carl Schachter [Schirmer]. In some ways it's a more approachable book than *Harmony*, but again, it's clear that the authors are writing entirely for the benefit of those whose primary goal is, if not actually to write music in the style of Mozart or Beethoven, at least to understand what Mozart and Beethoven and Brahms and Schumann were up to. Aldwell and Schachter are so nervous about anything resembling jazz harmony that in their discussion of 11th and 13th chords, they put the terms "11ths" and "13ths" in quotation marks, thereby refusing to grant such chords full legitimacy. They have a regrettable tendency to assert, rigidly and without qualification, that certain harmonic practices are "forbidden." And the word "jazz" is not to be found in their index. As valuable and coherent as their treatment of classical music theory is, it's hard to avoid the impression that they're a bit out of touch with what their students are actually playing down the hall in the practice room.

In *Chords & Harmony*, I've attempted to put together an overview of the subject that will be equally useful to aspiring pop, jazz, and classical musicians. Without going into nearly the depth of either of these monumental textbooks, I've tried to address the needs and answer the questions of several types of readers: younger musicians who are studying (or teaching themselves) guitar and other instruments in order to play pop music, older amateurs who would like to be able to play from the chord symbols in sheet music, DJs who may have no musical training but have started recording their own tracks, and — yes — classical musicians who may be very accomplished as instrumentalists but have little or no grounding in music theory, and who don't want to go back to school and sit in class month after month in order to improve their understanding.

In a very practical, no-nonsense way, *Chords & Harmony* covers the "other stuff" that gets skipped in most secondary school music programs and is often neglected by private teachers, most of whom focus on technique, interpretation, and literature rather than theory. Starting with the simplest concepts, this book builds a conceptual framework that will enable you both to understand what's going on harmonically in the music you play and to create your own music with greater confidence. Intervals, simple and complex chords, scales — all of the basic materials of harmony theory are described in these pages.

While *Chords & Harmony* will help you understand music theory at a very practical level, it's not a book of rules. Before we go any further, I want to make it clear that *there are no rules*. At any time, you're entirely free to play any combination of notes that sounds good to you. Some of the most exciting new styles in music — indeed, most of them — have developed when musicians tossed the old, tired ideas of the previous generation overboard and sailed merrily on, making joyful noises that shocked and offended their elders.

Nonetheless, some useful ideas about music have evolved in the European/American mainstream within the last 300 years. If you want to do things your own way, perhaps in the *hope* that you'll shock and offend older listeners while exciting your peers, it may prove useful to know what the old fogeys are expecting so you can do something different. And if you're planning to play with other musicians in anything but a strictly classical setting, you'll find it all but indispensable to have a common language with which you can talk about chords.

This book is about the common harmonic language of music. That is, it's about the theory and practice of harmony that has evolved in the so-called "common practice" period, which began about 1700 and ended, in the classical music world, about 1915. In the early 20th century, classical composers threw out many of the harmonic ideas that their predecessors had adhered to. With a few exceptions, such as fourth-chords and bitonalism, those experiments are not discussed in this book. The harmonic language pioneered by jazz musicians in the period between 1920 and 1950, however, is still directly relevant today, and is covered in some detail.

The book is designed for independent study by musicians who don't have a teacher, but it can also be used in the classroom. If you already know some music theory, please feel free to jump around and dip into whatever chapter looks interesting. If you're hoping to develop a thorough understanding of the subject matter, however, I'd suggest going through the chapters in order. Each chapter builds on the concepts introduced in previous chapters, so if you find yourself getting confused, you'd be well advised to turn back a few pages and study the earlier material a bit more.

—*Jim Aikin*

# ACKNOWLEDGMENTS

This book would be incomplete without a huge thank-you to Owen Goldsmith, whose inspiring curriculum at Livermore High School in the the mid-1960s included a full year of music theory. I'd also like to thank Tom Darter and the other editors of *Keyboard* magazine, who allowed me to write a number of tutorial features on music theory, and the readers who wrote to tell me how useful they found the articles.

Tom's contributions to *Chords & Harmony* as an editor were also invaluable. In the absence of his encyclopedic knowledge and his careful scrutiny of my explanations and musical examples, this book would have gone to press with a couple of glaring errors. Needless to say, any mistakes that remain are entirely my responsibility.

*—JA*

# 1
# GETTING STARTED

**P**laying music is one of the most complex human activities. It's partly a matter of athletics, involving physical strength, endurance, and the rapid-fire coordination of muscle, nerve, and tendon. It's partly a matter of pure emotion: Music that doesn't connect with listeners' feelings is of limited value. And yet passion and physical agility by themselves are not enough. To play music well, you also need a thorough working knowledge of a great many basic facts.

This book is not about the athletic part of music. Nor is it primarily about the emotional part, though we'll use emotion-laden terms from time to time when describing sounds. It's about some of the facts musicians need to know. Not all of the things they need to know, to be sure. You won't find any discussion of rhythm, dynamics, acoustics, history, arranging techniques, recording technology, group improvisation, performance skills, or the business side of music. In these pages we'll be concerned exclusively with harmony theory.

Some musicians, even some who are quite accomplished, may be unsure why they would need to know about chords and harmony. Isn't it enough to play well – to translate the dots on the page into accurate finger movements or tear through a hot solo that leaves the crowd gasping? Why plod through such dull stuff?

My answer is this: Trying to play music without knowing harmony theory is like driving a car while wearing a blindfold. If someone sits beside you and tells you when to turn and when to hit the brakes, you may be able to make it to the supermarket and back without trouble – but not only will you be dependent on another person, you'll miss out on a lot of scenery!

In the same way, you can get along for a while without knowing harmony theory. If you're content to play sheet music notated by others (as many classical musicians are), you may be able to play at a fairly high level and get a lot of satisfaction out of music simply by playing the written notes. But ultimately, understanding the harmonic underpinnings of what you're playing will give you a far deeper appreciation of the repertoire. To take a slightly different scenario, if you're into head-banging three-chord rock or one-chord hip-hop, you've probably had the experience of hearing a record and saying to yourself, "How did they *do* that? Why does that one note get me in the gut? How can I get that feeling into my next tune?" More often than you might expect, the way to find the answer is to develop a better understanding of harmony theory.

Some musicians have a positive aversion to learning theory. They're afraid it will get in the way of the pure, direct feeling of their music. But this doesn't have to be a problem. Yes, when you start adding a knowledge of theory to the things you already know intuitively, you'll have to go through a period of conscious mental effort as you struggle to assimilate it all. Work will be required. But once you've done the work, you'll find that you have a level of freedom and confidence that you lacked before. Your intuition will have a whole bunch of new toys to play with.

Theory should be worn as a loose garment. The way I look at it, the feeling of the music is always the primary thing. When theory starts getting in the way of the feeling, by all means toss the theory overboard without a moment's regret. As Thelonious Monk is supposed to have said, "There are no wrong notes." The point of knowing theory is not to place more restrictions on your music but to open up new possibilities.

Theory, to use a slightly different metaphor, is a road map. It will show you how to get to some interesting places, places you may never have known about before, or may have seen but only from a distance. You might have found your way to the same place eventually just by driving around, taking turns at random. But even after you stumble onto a wonderful view or a cozy little bed-and-breakfast, you may have trouble finding your way back again later if you don't have a map.

This book is your road map through the land of harmony. What sort of trip you take is entirely up to you.

## HOW TO STUDY THIS BOOK

In order to provide printed musical examples in this book, I have to make the assumption that you can read standard music notation. If you can't read music, or if you read a little but you're rusty, please turn to Appendix A, "How to Read Music."

I'm also going to assume that you have access to a musical instrument that can play chords. The best way to study the examples in this book — the only way, really — is sitting at a piano; reading about chords is no substitute for hearing them. If you don't have access to a piano that's in reasonable condition and has been tuned within living memory, an electronic keyboard (preferably one that has a decent piano sound) will do as a substitute. If you don't have a keyboard of any kind, you can attempt to play the examples on a guitar, but playing even some fairly standard chord voicings on a guitar (voicing, as explained later in this book, is the process of choosing particular combinations of notes to play together) can pose peculiar problems. If your primary instrument is guitar, I recommend that you find a keyboard instrument on which to study the materials in this book. Picking out one note at a time is okay: You don't need to become a keyboard whiz.

Ultimately, learning the language of harmony is a matter of training your ears — first to identify chords and intervals when you hear them, and then to imagine what they'll sound like *before* you hear them. Grabbing sophisticated chords and throwing them together at random, without the guidance of your ear, is an amusing game, but it's unlikely to be satisfying for very long. You may find it helpful to study this book with a more knowledgeable friend who can give you some practice in ear-training.

Ask your friend to play intervals on the keyboard (while you're not looking at it), and attempt to identify them by name. That is, don't worry about which notes are in the interval — perhaps E and C♯. Just give the name of the interval — in this case, a major 6th. As you get more comfortable identifying intervals, ask your friend to play various types of triads. Again, identifying the root of the triad — as a D major triad, for instance — is not important. Your goal is to be able to hear the difference between major, minor, diminished, and augmented triads. When you've mastered triads, proceed to 7th chords, and so on.

Each chapter ends with a brief quiz on the material covered in the chapter. The answers to the quiz questions are found in Appendix C. If you're using *Chords & Harmony* in a classroom setting, doubtless your teacher will want to expand on these quizzes.

Most of the information in the rest of Chapter One is quite basic — stuff you probably learned in your first or second year of music lessons. It builds a firm foundation for what follows. I like to be thorough, so I don't want to skip over this material. If you already know what key signatures, accidentals, and enharmonic equivalents are, you're probably ready to jump ahead to Chapter Two.

## THE ELEMENTS OF MUSIC

Music consists of sound. Other elements, such as lighting, costumes, dancing, and smoke bombs, are sometimes combined with the sound in a musical performance, but in general we think of the sound part of the performance as being the music, and the other elements as being theatre or multimedia. In another book (*Power Tools for Synthesizer Programming*) I've discussed the nature of sound in some detail. For the purposes of this book, we're going to take a more basic, pragmatic approach. Musical sound is made up of four aspects or components. All four are present in all music (unlike the dancing and the smoke bombs, which may or may not be part of a given piece), and making music is the process of combining them in various ways. The four components of music are pitch, rhythm, loudness, and tone color.

Together, these components form a type of language. While the language has no words, it does have the ability to express feelings and ideas. Like other languages, it has syntax. That is, there are recognized ways of putting together larger groupings called phrases and sections (the musical equivalent of sentences and paragraphs) out of smaller groupings called notes and chords (the musical equivalent of words). And as with other languages, the syntax of music is somewhat artificial and contains numerous bits that are the result of historical accidents.

The language of music works because it's shared. That is, everyone who listens to any appreciable amount of music in the European/American tradition quickly learns that certain combinations of sound belong together, and are used to say specific types of things. Other combinations are seldom used, and listeners don't find them especially meaningful. Whether they're not used because listeners don't find them meaningful, or whether listeners don't find them meaningful because they're so seldom used, is a chicken-or-egg problem, and I'm not going to try to make an omelette out of it here. Suffice it to say, the purpose of this book is to help you learn to speak one particular dialect or subset of the language of music, the subset that has to do with using pitches.

Before we get into that, though, perhaps we should touch quickly on the other three elements. They're far too important to ignore entirely, but they're not what this book is about.

Tone color is mainly determined by the choice of instruments being used. A trumpet and a violin, for instance, can play the same melody (the same pitches and rhythms, in other words). We can tell which instrument we're hearing because each has its own characteristic tone color. Likewise, a snare drum and a bongo drum — or, for that matter, a trash can lid — can play the same rhythm: We can tell which one we're hearing because their tone colors are different. Some instruments, such as synthesizers, can produce an incredible variety of tone colors, while others have a much more restricted range of available colors.

Loudness is important in various ways. If you start a piece by playing softly and then increase the volume, for instance, your listeners will tend to perceive the increase in volume as an increase in emotional intensity. But all things considered, loudness is pretty simple.

The word "rhythm" refers to the way musical events are positioned in time — whether they're close together or far apart, whether they're spaced evenly or unevenly, and whether they're arranged randomly or in some perceptible pattern. Rhythm is as interesting a subject as tone color, but again, it's not something that will be covered in this book.

Most of what we'll be discussing comes under the heading of pitch. So the very first thing we need to do is figure out just what we mean by "pitch." What is it, and how do we tell the difference between one pitch and another?

## PITCH

Musical pitch is closely related to *frequency*. The two are not identical, but for most purposes we can treat the terms as interchangeable. Whenever you play a musical instrument, you produce vibrations in the air. Most of the time, the vibrations are so close together that you won't perceive them as separate events. Instead, they'll blend together into a more or less continuous stream. When this stream of vibrations reaches your eardrum, you hear a sound. The speed of the vibrations — how frequent they are, in other words — is the frequency of the sound.

Consider a guitar string. When you pluck the string, it wobbles back and forth. In other words, it vibrates. The vibrations pass through the bridge of the instrument into the body if it's an acoustic guitar, or through a pickup, amp, and speakers if it's an electric. Either the body of the guitar or the speaker cones cause the air to vibrate, and the vibrations in the air are what you hear.

If the guitar string is stretched tightly, it will vibrate rapidly. If you turn the tuning peg so that the string is looser, it will vibrate more slowly. If you turn the peg so that the string is very loose indeed, you may even be able to see the string flopping back and forth, but in a normal musical situation it will be moving so rapidly that it will appear to be just a blur.

In general, objects that are smaller and/or more rigid produce more rapid vibrations, while things that are larger and/or looser produce slower vibrations. If you're curious about the effect of size on vibrations, take a peek inside an acoustic piano. The strings at one end of the piano frame are much shorter than the strings at the other end.

If the sound vibrations, whether they're coming from a guitar string or any other vibrating medium, are fast, we say they have a *high* frequency (that is, a high pitch). When they're slower, we say they have a *low* frequency (a low pitch).

Beginning guitarists and cellists are sometimes confused by this usage of the words "high" and "low." On a guitar, the high-pitched strings are physically lower (closer to the floor) when the instrument is held in normal playing position. On a cello or acoustic bass, because the strings run vertically, higher notes are played by stopping the strings with the fingers in a physically lower position (again, closer to the floor). It's important to understand that pitch height is a metaphor: It has nothing to do with physical height.

While standing in front of a piano, play a key near the left end (where the strings are long) and a key near the right end (where the strings are short) and listen to the differences in sound. Some of the differences are due to the fact that the high notes of a piano die away more quickly than the low notes, but in any event you should be able to perceive a clear difference in pitch between the two notes.

Next, play two notes that are closer together – perhaps near the middle of the keyboard – and compare their pitches with your inner ear. The very first thing you need to learn as a musician is how to tell when one pitch is higher or lower than another. If you love music but you can't tell high from low, your only hope is to become a drummer.

This book won't contain any more drummer jokes, that's a promise. This one isn't even a good joke, because drummers routinely tune their drums to higher and lower pitches. But there's a serious point behind the joke. Most musical instruments produce tones that have clear and distinct pitches. This is true of all wind and string instruments, and it's also true of tuned percussion instruments such as piano, marimba, xylophone, and timpani. Other percussion instruments, such as drums and cymbals, produce tones whose pitch is much less distinct. A snare drum can be tuned much like a guitar string, so it makes sense to talk about a snare drum as having a high or low pitch – but because the sound of the drum is so filled with noise, it's not generally possible to say exactly what the pitch of the drum is.

We're getting a little ahead of ourselves. Pitches, you see, have names. Later in this chapter we'll explain how pitches are named. First, though, we need to explore a few other aspects of the pitch/frequency spectrum.

## PLAYING IN TUNE

One of the curious facts about pitch is that while the frequency spectrum provides an infinite number of different pitches, our musical tradition uses only a relatively small, fixed set of pitches. Most of the pitches that we might play (accidentally or on purpose) fall "in the cracks" between the pitches of the conventional musical scale. We'll have very little to say in this book about those in-between pitches. You do need to understand that they exist, however, if only so that you'll be able to judge when an instrumentalist or vocalist is playing or singing in tune.

What exactly do we mean by "in tune," and how does it differ from "out of tune"? If your instrument is the piano or some other type of keyboard, you may never need to worry about this question, because someone else will tune your instrument for you (if it needs to be tuned at all). But most musicians wrestle with tuning every day, and most instruments require that the performer be aware of the intonation of each note. "Intonation" is more or less a fancy word for "tuning," but the words are used in slightly different ways. The difference is that the instrument itself has to be tuned, while each note has to be played or sung with the correct intonation.

When two tones are sounded at the same time and have precisely the same pitch, they tend to blend together into a composite tone. This is especially true if they have similar tone colors, and if they start at about the same time. If their pitches are close but not quite the same, there will be a clash. The technical term for this clash is *beating*. Beating is perceived as a sort of "wah-wah-wah" effect. Beats are easiest to hear when the two tones sustain for a reasonable period of time.

The beats are actually *difference tones*, which are caused by the difference in frequency between the two tones. For instance, if one tone has a fundamental frequency of 440Hz while the other has a frequency of 438Hz, the difference between the two numbers is 2Hz. In this case, if the two tones are sounded simultaneously you'll hear beats at a rate of two per second. (Note: "Hz" is an abbreviation for "Hertz," which means the same thing as "cycles per second." So a tone with a frequency of 440Hz is vibrating at a rate of 440 cycles per second.)

Beats are easier to hear than to describe in words. If you have access to a guitar, by all means try listening to beats for yourself. Place a finger behind the fifth fret of the B string (the second-highest string) and play both this string and the open E string (the highest string) at the same time, allowing them to ring for a few seconds. Then retune the E string either up or down slightly using its tuning gear and play the two notes again. At a certain point, when the two notes are in tune with one another, the sound will be very smooth. If they're not tuned to the same pitch, the beats will be more or less apparent.

If you're playing an instrument that you have to tune yourself, and especially if you're playing an instrument such as violin, cello, or trombone, which has no keys, valves, or frets to help guide you to the correct pitches, learning to hear when your instrument is in tune with some reference pitch (such as the tuning note played by the oboe in an orchestra) is a vital part of musicianship. Pitch perception is also essential to hearing and identifying the two-note combinations discussed in Chapter Two.

When two tones are fairly close to one another in pitch, we can use the terms *flat* and *sharp* to describe their pitch relationship. The higher of the two tones is sharp in relation to the lower tone, while the lower tone is flat in relation to the higher tone:

sharp = higher
flat = lower

Figure 1-1. Examples of musical lines. Examples (a) and (b) are most likely melodies. Example (c) shows two independent lines notated on one staff; the top line is the melody, while the bottom line is counterpoint. Example (d) is a type of bass line. This is clear not only because it's in the bass clef, but because the pattern of notes is typical of certain old-time rock and roll styles.

We'll meet these two terms again when we start talking about scales and accidentals. They refer to half-step relationships within the scale, and also to tuning adjustments that are smaller than a half-step.

## LINES, INTERVALS & CHORDS

Broadly speaking, musical sounds can be played one after another, or they can be played at the same time.

When two or more pitched sounds are played one after another, they're called a *line*. Melody lines (also known as melodies) and bass lines (usually the lowest notes in a piece of music) are the types of lines people usually think of first, but *counterpoint* lines are also extremely common. Counterpoint is a type of writing in which two or more independent lines are played or sung at the same time. For some examples of lines, see Figure 1-1. Unpitched sounds, such as drum parts, are not usually referred to as lines.

Another term that's more or less synonymous with "line" is *voice*. When two or more notes are played in a series, we say they're being played by the same

why we use these names. The white keys each have a simple letter name (A, B, C, D, E, F, G) while the black keys can have either of two different names (see "Enharmonic Equivalents," below). As Figure 1-5 shows, this arrangement is repeated up and down the keyboard: Every group of 12 pitches has the same names as in the groups above and below it.

To look at it a slightly different way, we can say that the frequency spectrum is divided up into 12 groups of pitches called *pitch classes*, each of which contains seven or eight elements. All of the notes with the name C, for example, belong to the same pitch class. Figure 1-6 illustrates the idea of pitch classes.

Before going any further, we should note that in one sense, the set of frequencies we use, which is called the *equal-tempered 12-note chromatic scale*, is entirely arbitrary. We could as easily divide the frequency spectrum up in some other way. The number of potential scales (also called tuning systems) is infinite. But there are powerful pragmatic reasons why the chromatic scale musicians use every day is laid out as it is. I've included a fuller explanation of this in Appendix B, "The Harmonic Series and Equal Temperament."

As noted above, pitched sounds vibrate at specific, discrete frequencies. Our ears are remarkably good at figuring out — at least in an intuitive sense — how rapidly the vibrations are occurring. We can't actually count the separate vibrations in a tone that's vibrating at a frequency of more than 10 or 12 cycles per sec-

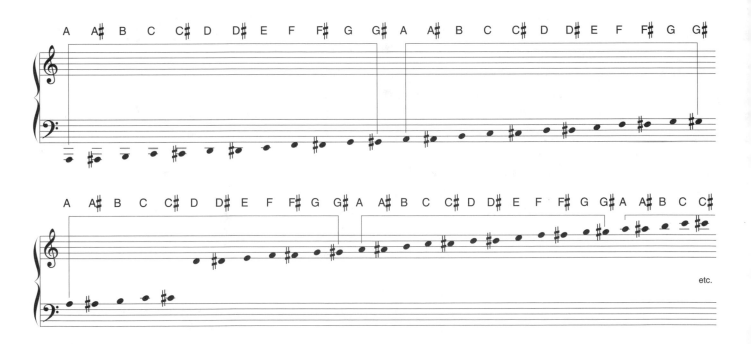

Figure 1-5. One way to look at the chromatic scale is as a repeating series of 12-note groups, each of which contains the notes from A up to G♯. Only a portion of the full chromatic scale is shown here; it extends both upward and downward.

Figure 1-6. In place of the grouping in Figure 1-4, we can look at the chromatic scale as consisting of 12 groups, each of which contains all of the notes that have the same letter-name. Here we see the grouped A's, A#'s, and B's. As in Figure 1-4, only a portion of each group is shown; the dotted lines indicate that the groups extend both upward and downward.

ond, but some people can learn to identify tones that have specific frequencies, such as 440 cycles per second (a talent called "perfect pitch"), and most people can learn to identify relationships among frequencies (a talent called "relative pitch"). Those who are unable to do so even in a rudimentary way are referred to as tone-deaf.

The easiest relationship to identify is when the frequency of one tone is the same as the frequency of another tone. As explained above in the section on "Playing In Tune," this relationship is called a *unison*. "Unison" is in fact a Latin-derived word that means "one sound."

After the unison, the next easiest relationship for our ears to identify is when the frequency of one tone is twice or half the frequency of another. This relationship is called the *octave*. "Octave" comes from a Latin word that means "eight," a fact that will make more sense when we've covered a little more ground.

Tones that are an octave apart are felt to be so similar that they have the same name. If you're sitting in front of a piano, try playing all of the C keys, one at a time, from the bottom of the keyboard to the top. Assuming your piano is in tune, you should be able to sense the strong similarity among these tones. The lowest C on the piano has a frequency of about 32.7032Hz, and the frequency of each C as you progress up the keyboard is exactly twice this number, as shown in Figure 1-7.

If it seems odd to you that a nice, familiar note like C doesn't have a nice, round number for a frequency, you're right: It *is* odd. Many aspects of music, including the pitch of C, are based on traditions that have evolved over the centuries, not on common sense. The essential point is that the frequency doubles as we move up an octave — or, to look at it the other way, the frequency is cut in half each time we drop an octave.

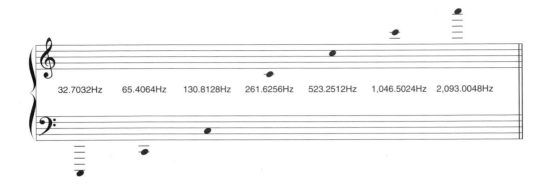

*Figure 1-7. Each note in the chromatic scale has twice the frequency of the note with the same name that's an octave below it. To look at it another way, doubling the frequency of a tone raises it by one octave. Shown here are the actual frequencies in Hz (cycles per second) of the note C in seven octaves.*

This is true for each of the notes on the keyboard. The A above Middle C has a frequency of 440Hz. The A below Middle C has a frequency of 220Hz, the A below that is at 110Hz, and so on. There's not much point in going any lower than the bottom A (27.5Hz) on the piano keyboard, because this is close to the lower threshold of humans' ability to hear pitch.

If you count the keys on the keyboard between any note and the note an octave higher or lower, you'll find that (not including the octave repetition of the starting note) there are exactly 12 notes within any given octave. This is true no matter what note you choose as your starting point, as Figure 1-5 makes clear. Each octave of the chromatic scale is exactly like every other octave.

As Figure 1-4 shows, the white keys on the piano have letter-names: A, B, C, D, E, F, and G. There are seven of these notes, and they repeat in every octave. Starting with E, for instance, and proceeding up the keyboard using only the white keys, the seventh note is D. The next note, another E an octave above the first, is the *eighth* note. That's why octaves are called octaves — the term refers to the layout of white keys, not to the chromatic scale as a whole. If the term were derived from the 12-tone chromatic scale, we'd have to describe the interval in which the frequency is doubled or halved using the word "duodecimatives" or something equally horrible.

The layout of notes on the staff perfectly reflects the white-key layout of the keyboard: Each white key has its own line or space (see Figure 1-8). The black keys don't.

The keyboard and notation system we use today originated in the Middle Ages. Originally, the white keys were the only keys that existed. That's the main reason why the naming convention uses only seven letters. As time went on, com-

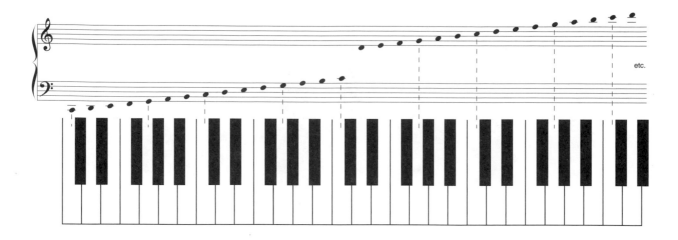

*Figure 1-8. The layout of lines and spaces on the staff reflects the layout of the piano keyboard. Each white key gets its own line or space.*

posers found it useful to add a few notes that were "in the cracks" between the white keys. Shorter keys, positioned above the main row of keys, were added. Some early keyboards didn't have five of these shorter keys in every octave; they only had two or three. Later, in the Renaissance, keyboards were sometimes built with *more* than five of the shorter keys. The F♯/G♭ key, for instance, might be a "split" key, which allowed the performer to play either of two slightly different pitches between F and G. The layout we have today is an effective compromise: There are enough keys to allow us to play a wide variety of chords and melodies, but not so many that playing the keyboard turns into a knuckle-banging nightmare.

The fact that the relationships among white keys are considered basic, while the black keys were added on afterward, accounts for some other important bits of terminology. The distance between two adjacent white keys that have a black key between them is called a *whole-step* (see Figure 1-9). The relationship between any white key and the black key that lies next to it is called a *half-step*. In fact, there's nothing particularly "whole" about a whole-step. If you play guitar, it will be obvious that this entire naming convention — letter-names, whole-steps, and half-steps — is more than a bit arbitrary, because on a guitar the basic unit of the scale is the half-step (a distance of one fret up or down). The only way to play a note that's half a fret away from another note is by bending the string, an action that takes you entirely outside the scale we're talking about.

Another term for half-step is *semitone*. "Semi-" is a Latin prefix that means "half." The corresponding term for a whole-step would be "tone," but except in a few textbooks the word is no longer used in this way — except in one particular instance. The interval of an augmented fourth or diminished fifth, which we'll

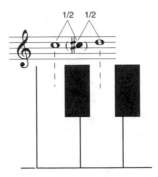

*Figure 1-9. A whole-step (in this case, from C to D), contains two half-steps (in this case, C to C♯ and C♯ to D).*

meet in Chapter Two, is called a *tritone*, a term that means "three tones." A tritone consists of three intervals, each a tone in width, stacked one on top of the other.

The other term that derives from the keyboard layout is *accidental*. The black keys were not originally felt to be an entirely legitimate part of the scale, the way the white keys were. They were sort of harmonic accidents. This term has a more direct meaning in terms of key signatures, which we'll get to below. But if you think of the black keys as being accidental in terms of the scale you hear when you play the white keys, you'll be right on the money.

## DO-RE-MI

If you play the white keys on the keyboard, starting at C and playing each key until you arrive back at C, you'll produce a familiar-sounding scale. This is called the *major* scale, because the first and third notes (C and E) form the interval of a major 3rd. We'll take a more systematic look at this interval, and how it relates to other intervals, in Chapter Two.

If you look at the arrangement of white and black keys on the keyboard (see Figure 1-10), you'll see that the major scale is made up of a pattern of whole-steps and half-steps. This pattern (two whole-steps followed by a half-step, and then three more whole-steps followed by another half-step) is what defines the major scale. Other scales can be built by combining whole-steps and half-steps in different ways. We'll look at some of the more useful alternatives in Chapter Seven.

As long as you keep the arrangement of whole-steps and half-steps the same, you can build a major scale by starting on any note in the chromatic scale. The note on which the scale starts is called the *tonic*, because it provides a reference point for the *tonality* of the music. Another term for the same concept is *key*. When the major scale starts and ends on the note D, for example, we say that it's in the key of D, and that D is the tonic.

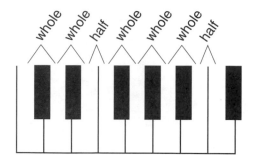

*Figure 1-10. The pattern of whole-steps and half-steps in the C major scale.*

In addition to their letter-names, the notes in the major scale have another set of names, which are also shown in Figure 1-11 — do, re, mi, fa, so, la, and ti. (In Europe, "do" is also known as "ut," and "ti" is sometimes called "si." "Sol" is an alternative for "so," but because it's followed by "la," the final "l" sometimes gets dropped.) Many young music students learn these nonsense syllables in grade school. The syllables have one advantage over the letter-names for the notes: Do, re, mi, and the other names are the same no matter what note the scale starts on.

## KEY SIGNATURES & ACCIDENTALS

Since the major scale is used in so much of our music, and since our tuning system so conveniently allows us to start a major scale on any note of the chromatic scale, music is often full of notes that are played on the black keys of the keyboard. Maybe you can imagine how messy it would be if, each time we encountered an A in sheet music, the sheet music had to indicate whether we were to play an A♭ (the black key below A), an A♯ (the black key above A), or an A♮ (the white key). To make music easier to read, this information is placed not within each measure but at the beginning of each staff.

*Figure 1-11. The notes of the major scale have nonsense names. (In Europe, "do" is often referred to as "ut," and "so" is "sol"). These names are the same no matter what key the music is in; they're shown here with a C major scale purely for convenience. "Do" always refers to the tonic, "re" to the 2nd step of the scale, and so on.*

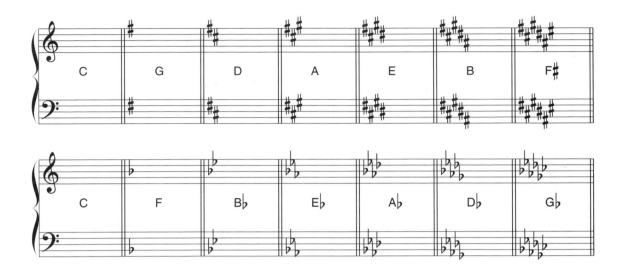

Figure 1-12. The key signatures of the major keys. The flats or sharps placed at the beginning of the staff (or after a double bar line, as shown here) indicate which notes on the staff are to be played a half-step higher or lower than the white key that would otherwise be played. In the key of D, for instance, all of the occurrences of the note F in the staff would be played as F♯, and all of the occurrences of C would be played as C♯.

In sheet music, whenever the music is in a key other than C, a *key signature* (a group of one or more sharps or flats) is found at the beginning of each staff. The key signature tells you which notes to raise or lower by a half-step in order to produce a major scale. It's placed at the beginning of each staff, and applies to all of the notes of that pitch class that are found anywhere in the staff, whether or not they're in the same octave as the accidental in the key signature. The basic key signatures are shown in Figure 1-12, and Figure 1-13 shows how to interpret a key signature.

Figure 1-13. The key signature with three flats indicates that the music is in the key of E♭ major — or possibly in the relative minor of E♭ major, which is C minor. Relative minor keys are discussed in Chapter Four. When this key signature is used, an E♭ major scale can be written using no accidentals, as in (a). When no key signature is used (b), the same scale has to be written using an accidental before the first occurrence of any E♭, A♭, or B♭ in any measure.

There are a few pieces of modern music whose key signatures include both flats and sharps, but we can safely ignore these. Note also that in some sheet music prepared by arrangers for recording sessions, the key signature is shown not at the beginning of each staff but only at the beginning of the piece. The assumption is that the people reading the sheet music will be professionals, and will be able to remember what key they're playing in.

Whenever the composer or arranger needs to temporarily cancel one of the flats or sharps in the key signature, an accidental (a flat, sharp, or natural, or more rarely a double-sharp or double-flat) is placed before the note that is to be altered. Looking at it a slightly different way, an accidental is not the flat, sharp, or natural in the sheet music but rather a note that isn't included in the major scale indicated by the current key signature. In the key of E♭, for example, an A♮ (a white key) would be an accidental.

Each key signature is referred to by the name of the tonic note of the major scale that can be played using that key signature without inserting any accidentals. For instance, if the key signature allows us to play a D major scale with no accidentals — that is, if it contains exactly two sharps — it's the D major key signature.

In symphonic music, the key signature may change a number of times in the course of a single piece. This happens when the music *modulates* to a new key (a subject we'll have more to say about in Chapter Eight). Composers change the key signature in order to make a passage easier for the musicians to read. It's easier to read because fewer accidentals are required to notate it. On the down side, it becomes necessary to make a mental note of the current key signature at all times.

## MAJOR KEYS, SCALES & THE CIRCLE OF FIFTHS

Because there are 12 notes in the chromatic scale, it's possible to play a major scale in any of 12 different keys. For reference, Figure 1-14 shows all 12 of these scales. Assuming you know how to read music, you may be more used to seeing the scales written with key signatures. In Figure 1-14, however, I've notated them without key signatures, using accidentals, as this makes it easier to see how various notes are raised or lowered.

The arrangement of keys in Figures 1-12 and 1-14 is not random or capricious: The scales are arranged in an order called the *Circle of Fifths*. The Circle of Fifths is so important that it deserves a brief explanation here. We'll have more to say about it in Chapter Five.

Studying Figures 1-12 and 1-14 is a worthwhile exercise. As you examine them, you'll notice some patterns. When we add a sharp or remove a flat, for instance, the note that's affected is the note just below the tonic. As we transition from the key of A to the key of E, for instance, the note D (one step below E) changes to a D♯. See if you can figure out which note of the scale is lowered by a half-step when the key signature moves the other direction, for example from the key of C to the key of F, or from F to B♭. (Note also that these Figures show only the *major* keys. The subject of minor keys will have to wait until Chapter Four.)

*Figure 1-14. The major scales, written without key signatures. If the key signatures shown in Figure 1-12 were used, the scales here would look a lot alike: They'd all be simple rows of notes, with no accidentals. Note that the scales of F♯ major and G♭ major contain exactly the same chromatic pitches. However, each pitch is spelled using one of two enharmonic equivalents: F♯ is the same note as G♭, G♯ is the same as A♭, and so on.*

When a piece of music originally written in one key is moved up or down in pitch so that it's in a different key, we say that the music has been *transposed*. Transposing music to a new key is often necessary so that a vocalist can sing the melody without straining.

Transposition doesn't mean simply slapping a new key signature on an existing bunch of notes. If we did that, the melody and harmony would most likely sound very strange. Instead, all of the notes are moved up or down by some number of half-steps so that the tonic note (for example, G in the key of G major) lands on the tonic of the new key (for example, E♭ in the key of E♭). All of the other notes in the piece are moved up or down by the same number of half-steps, with the result that the music sounds exactly the way it did before, only higher or lower.

## ENHARMONIC EQUIVALENTS

Look again at Figure 1-14. If you play the F♯ and G♭ scales on a keyboard (or, for that matter, on a guitar or any other instrument) you'll find that you're using exactly the same notes, even though the two scales look completely different on the page. In fact, this is an extreme instance of a more general phenomenon: Many other notes found in two different scales are spelled differently while sounding the same — for instance, the D♯ in the B major scale is the same note as the E♭ in the B♭ major scale. What's unique about the scales of F♯ and G♭ is that *all* of the notes are the same, but spelled differently.

Notes that sound and are played the same, but are spelled differently, are called *enharmonic equivalents*. The word "spell" in this case refers simply to the choice of which letter we use to refer to the note. As we move into more advanced harmonic territory, we'll encounter many enharmonic equivalents.

The fact that a given note can be spelled two different ways may seem at first to be merely an inconvenience. Why can't we always call a given note by a single name, and be done with it? (In fact, I've met a few guitarists who do exactly this. To them, the note a half-step above C is always D♭, never C♯.) There's an important reason for it, however. When notating scales, we want the scale to look sensible on the page, with one scale step per line or space on the staff. For instance, in the A scale, the notes A, B, C♯, and D follow one another in a neat line. If we were to spell the third note as D♭, then the A scale would contain the notes A, B, D♭, and D. There would be two D's in the scale, and no C. This would make reading sheet music quite difficult. What would we use for a key signature? Would we put a flat on the line for the D, or not?

A system in which the black keys on the keyboard can be referred to with the letter-name of either the white key below them (as a sharp) or the white key above them (as a flat) gives us a clear, concise way to notate and talk about all of the scales, chords, and intervals that are commonly used.

*Figure 1-15. Enharmonic equivalents. Each pair of notes shown here produces the same pitch. Notes like E♯ and C♭ are not often needed; they're only used in keys that already have lots of sharps or flats in the key signature.*

The F♯ and G♭ scales illustrate another concept that will be useful from time to time. While a sharp or flat note is normally one of the black keys on the keyboard, this is not always the case. Remember that making a note sharp simply means raising it by a half-step. When we raise the note E or B by a half-step to E♯ or B♯, we land on another white key (F or C respectively). So E♯ and F are enharmonic equivalents. The same thing is true of B♯ and C, F♭ and E, and C♭ and B (see Figure 1-15).

## QUIZ *

1. What are the four basic elements of music?
2. Which major key has four sharps in the key signature? Which major key has two flats?
3. What is the relationship between two pitches called?
4. What is a set of three or more notes played together called?
5. What is the enharmonic equivalent of A♭? Of D♭? Of C?
6. What is a unison?
7. What instrument is the arpeggio named for?
8. When two notes are almost in tune, but not quite, playing them together produces a clash. What is the technical term for the sound of this clash?

* For answers to the quizzes, see page 185.

# 2

# INTERVALS

In order to work with chords and harmony, you have to start by developing a clear understanding of intervals. Intervals are the building blocks out of which all of the more complex phenomena of harmony are built. An interval, as explained in Chapter One, is simply a relationship between two notes.

Technically, an intervallic relationship is between pitches, not notes. A note is a musical entity that has a pitch and also a duration. For instance, it might be an eighth-note with a pitch of E♭. Notes, even if they're written on paper and never heard, are intended to be played, while pitches are abstractions. Most notes also have definite rhythmic positions within a piece of music, though of course it's possible to play one note in isolation. In this book, however, I'll generally use the more comfortable, familiar term. I'll refer to the elements of intervals and chords most often as notes, not as pitches.

We've already met several intervals in Chapter One: the unison, the octave, the 5th, the major 3rd, the half-step, and the whole-step. The time has come to define these terms in a more systematic way.

Figuring out the name of an interval is pretty easy: You do it by counting the number of scale steps between the lower and upper notes (including both of the notes in the count). This idea is shown in Figure 2-1.

The unison and octave could just as easily be called the 1st and 8th, but their special importance is highlighted by giving them special names. The two notes of a unison are the same. The two notes of an octave both have the same name (C and C, in Figure 2-1), and in many harmonic contexts are interchangeable, but they're

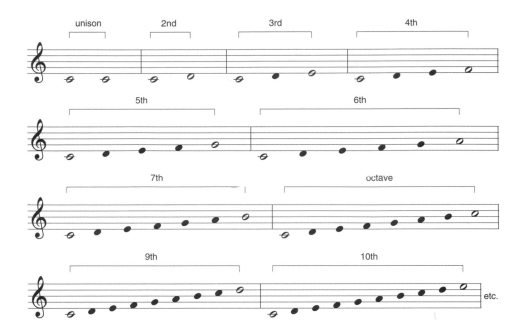

Figure 2-1. The names of intervals are based on how many steps of the scale are included within the span of the two notes of the interval. Both the top and bottom notes of the interval are counted in figuring out the name. In this diagram the notes of the scale between the two notes of the interval are shown as black noteheads, while the notes of the interval are shown as hollow noteheads.

not the same. If you're new to music, learning to hear the difference between two notes an octave apart may require a little effort, because they sound very similar.

Before moving on, you need to notice several things about Figure 2-1 that may not be obvious at first glance.

First, the interval of a 9th consists of two notes with the same note names (C and D) as the interval of a 2nd. Likewise, the 10th has the same note names as the 3rd. In essence, a 9th consists of a 2nd plus an octave, and a 10th consists of a 3rd plus an octave.

Since an octave spans eight notes, you might expect that when jumping up an octave you'd use the formula $2 + 8 = 10$ to find the name of the wider interval. But it doesn't work that way. Since the octave note (the upper C in Figure 2-1) is only counted once, you add an octave to an interval by adding seven to its name. For a 2nd, the formula is $2 + 7 = 9$. For a 3rd it's $3 + 7 = 10$. This idea is illustrated in Figure 2-2.

Second, to save space Figure 2-1 doesn't include any intervals larger than a 10th, but such intervals exist. Musicians seldom have need to refer by name to intervals larger than a 13th. With a very large interval, you'd be more likely to say something like, "Two octaves plus a 5th."

*Figure 2-2. To increase an interval by an octave, add 7 (not 8) to the name. A 2nd plus an octave equals a 9th; a 3rd plus an octave equals a 10th.*

Third, the name of the interval doesn't depend on the *order* of the two notes. For the sake of convenience and consistency, in this book we'll most often talk about intervals by stating the lower of the two notes first, but this is arbitrary. The interval from C up to G is the same as the interval from G down to C (but not the same as the interval from C down to G, as you'll soon learn).

Fourth, a C major scale has been used in Figure 2-1 purely for convenience, and the lower note of all the intervals is C. Many of the examples in this book will be given in the key of C, but all of the harmonic phenomena we'll be discussing can be transposed to any key. The intervals D-F, E-G, and so on are all 3rds, just as C-E is.

Finally, some important intervals seem to be missing from Figure 2-1. Where, for instance, is our good friend the half-step? Somewhere between the unison and the 2nd, it would seem. And what about the distance between C and A♭? What are we to call it? A system that didn't provide names for all of the intervals wouldn't be very useful. So the question of what to call those "in-between" intervals is what we'll turn to next.

## NARROWING & WIDENING THE INTERVALS

The concept I'm about to introduce may be hard to remember at first. It may seem arbitrary or nonsensical. In fact, it makes excellent sense, but for reasons that won't be fully explained until we get to Chapter Seven.

Within the major scale there are two kinds of steps. Some of the notes are called *tonal* steps and some are called *modal* steps. In each scale, the tonal steps are the tonic, the 4th, the 5th, and the octave (in the C scale, the notes C, F, G, and C). The other steps (the 2nd, 3rd, 6th, and 7th) are the modal steps. The same thing is true of steps in the second octave: The 9th and 10th are modal, the 11th and 12th tonal.

The reasoning behind these terms is that the modal steps change, depending on what mode you're using. (As explained in Chapter Seven, a mode is a type of scale.) The 3rd, for instance, will be lowered by a half-step when we change from a major scale to the minor scale that has the same tonic. The tonal steps remain fixed in most of the classical modes, though they're altered in some jazz scales.

Modal steps have two basic forms, which are called *major* (which is Latin for "bigger") and *minor* (Latin for "smaller"). Tonal steps have only one basic form, which is called *perfect* (that's English for "don't ever change"). If we count the number of half-steps in an interval instead of the number of scale steps, we'll find that a minor interval always has one fewer half-steps than its major counterpart. A minor 2nd, for example, is one half-step in width, while a major 2nd is two half-steps wide. These relationships are summarized in Figure 2-3 and Table 2-1.

*Figure 2-3. The perfect, major, and minor intervals. Play these intervals on a keyboard to hear how they sound, and count the number of half-steps within each interval.*

*Table 2-1. The perfect, major, and minor intervals.*

| interval | type | number of half-steps | example |
|---|---|---|---|
| perfect unison | tonal | 0 | C-C |
| minor 2nd | modal | 1 | C-D♭ |
| major 2nd | modal | 2 | C-D |
| minor 3rd | modal | 3 | C-E♭ |
| major 3rd | modal | 4 | C-E |
| perfect 4th | tonal | 5 | C-F |
| perfect 5th | tonal | 7 | C-G |
| minor 6th | modal | 8 | C-A♭ |
| major 6th | modal | 9 | C-A |
| minor 7th | modal | 10 | C-B♭ |
| major 7th | modal | 11 | C-B |
| perfect octave | tonal | 12 | C-C |
| minor 9th | modal | 13 | C-D♭ |
| major 9th | modal | 14 | C-D |
| etc. | | | |

As you look at Table 2-1, you'll notice right away that we've skipped something. What about the interval that consists of six half-steps? Don't worry — it has a name too, but that name requires a little more explanation. We can make tonal perfect intervals larger or smaller by adding or removing a half-step, just as we do with modal intervals. We have to use a different type of name, however. There's no such thing as a "major 5th" or "minor 5th," because the 5th step of the scale is the same whether we're playing in a major or minor mode. Instead, a 5th that has been narrowed by a half-step is called a *diminished 5th*. A 4th that has been enlarged by a half-step is called an *augmented 4th*. The interval containing six half-steps can be referred to either as a diminished 5th or as an augmented 4th, depending on how it's spelled. If the lower note of the interval is C and the upper note is F♯, the interval is called an augmented 4th, because the interval C-F contains four scale steps. But if we spell the upper note as a G♭, then the interval is called a diminished 5th, because it's looked at as being based on the interval C-G. These intervals are shown in Figure 2-4.

Figure 2-4. Between the perfect 4th and perfect 5th lies the tritone, which can be spelled either as an augmented 4th or a diminished 5th.

An interval that has two names? Isn't that an invitation to confusion? Well, yes, it is. If you look at it a slightly different way, however, the augmented 4th and diminished 5th are really different intervals. They just happen to have the same number of half-steps. To avoid the hassle of figuring out whether they're referring to a diminished 5th or augmented 4th in a particular instance, some people refer to this interval as a *tritone*. As mentioned in Chapter One, a tritone is an interval that spans three whole-steps.

The number of half-steps in an interval is not the decisive factor in what sort of name we give it. Setting aside oddball terms like "tritone," the factor that determines the name of an interval is, first and foremost, the distance between the letter-names of the two notes that form the interval. As long as the two notes are closer together than an octave, any interval that contains a C as the lower note and an E as the upper note, for instance, or a D as the lower note and an F as the upper note, is always some type of 3rd. Any interval that contains a C as the lower note and a G as the upper note (again, assuming the interval is smaller than an octave) is a 5th. And so on. Naturally, we don't have to use C as the lower note of the interval: An interval whose lower note is a D and whose upper note is an A (assuming they're in the same octave) is a 5th, as is the interval from an E up to a B. This idea is summarized in Figure 2-5.

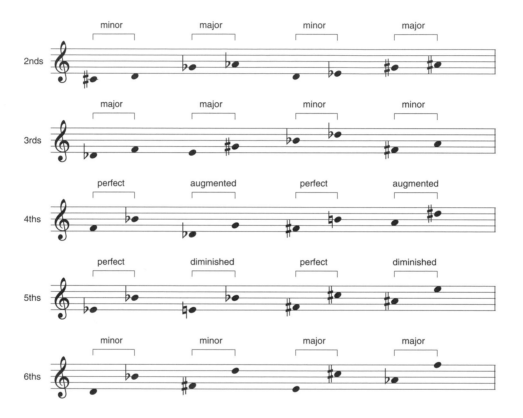

Figure 2-5. Even though the intervals shown here include accidentals, the name of the interval is still based on the distance between the letter-names of the notes (or, if you prefer, on how many lines and spaces separate the two notes on the staff). The type of interval (major, minor, augmented, or diminished) is based on the number of half-steps. To verify that the names given here are correct, locate these intervals on the keyboard and count the number of half-steps each of them spans.

# INTERVALS VS. SCALE STEPS & CHORD MEMBERS

We began by defining intervals in terms of scale steps. The interval between the first and third steps of the scale, for instance, is called a 3rd. It's important to understand that we're using three slightly different but closely related concepts here, which, sad to say, share the same names. Let's look at them one by one:

Within the C major scale, the E is the 3rd scale step, the F is the 4th scale step, and so on. Most of the discussion of scales and scale steps in this book is found in Chapter Seven.

Within a given chord, as explained in Chapter Three, each note has some relationship to the root. In a C major chord, the note E is called the 3rd. It's called that because the interval between C and E is a 3rd.

Finally, intervals themselves are referred to as 2nds, 3rds, 4ths, and so on. These names are used even when we aren't referring to any particular scale or chord, but simply to the interval between two notes.

Thus we can use the term "3rd" to refer to an interval, a scale step, or a note within a chord. The name of the scale step or chord note is the same as the name of the interval between that step or chord note and the tonic note of the scale or the root of the chord — but when we say, "The 3rd of an F chord is A," we're referring to the note A itself as a 3rd. We're not talking, at that moment, about the interval between F and A, which is also a 3rd. This is important, because when we start talking about chords, we'll often refer to the notes within a chord as 3rds, 5ths, and so on.

Even though there is only one 3rd scale step within a given scale (the note that is a 3rd above the tonic note of the scale), each scale contains a number of intervals of a 3rd. Within the C major scale, the interval from D to F is a 3rd (a minor 3rd, as it happens), from D to G is a 4th, and so on. All of the intervals in the C major scale that are smaller than an octave are shown in Figure 2-6. This figure also indicates which of these intervals are major, minor, augmented, and diminished. Being able to grasp the interval relationships within the scale is an important part of learning to use chords.

To reiterate, the terms "3rd," "5th," "7th," and so forth can refer to three distinct things: They're the names of intervals, and they're also the names of notes within a particular scale or chord. In the latter case, the name indicates the interval that lies between the note and the root of the chord or the tonic of the scale — the nearest root or tonic *below* the note, to be a little more specific. For example, in an A scale, the 5th is E, because the interval from A up to E is a 5th.

In some music theory texts, these two usages are formatted using different typography. You may see the names of pure intervals spelled out (as third, fourth, fifth, etc.), while the names of notes within a scale or chord are formatted as ordinal numerals (3rd, 4th, 5th, etc.). In this book, I've chosen to use numerals for both usages, on the theory that nobody but typographers and copyeditors pays much attention to the difference in formatting.

*Figure 2-6. Most of the examples earlier in this chapter use C as the lower note of the interval. Intervals can start on any note, however. Shown here are all of the intervals smaller than an octave that use the notes of the C major scale: 2nds (a), 3rds (b), 4ths (c), 5ths (d), 6ths (e), and 7ths (f). The type of each interval is shown. These interval relationships are the same in any major scale: For instance, if you start on the 2nd step of the scale and construct an interval of a 3rd, it will always be a minor 3rd.*

## MORE WAYS TO ALTER INTERVALS

If you're the type of person who likes to break the rules once in a while, you may look at Figure 2-5 and find yourself wondering, "What would happen if I made an interval by putting an E♭ next to an F♯? What sort of interval would that be? Or what if I combine a G♯ with a B♭?"

These are real intervals. Useful ones, too. They even have names. When a major/minor-type interval (one based on a modal scale step) is stretched by an extra half-step, so that it's even bigger than a major, it's referred to as an augmented interval — the same term we've already met when talking about perfect (tonal) intervals that are enlarged by a half-step. Likewise, when a modal interval is narrowed by an extra half-step, it's called diminished.

Thus there are not two types of 2nds, 3rds, 6ths, and 7ths, but four – diminished, minor, major, and augmented. And 4ths and 5ths can be either widened or narrowed, so there are actually three types of 4ths and 5ths – diminished, perfect, and augmented. The full panoply of possibilities is shown in Figure 2-7.

Figure 2-7. A more complete catalog of intervals, with a couple of examples of most types. Doubly augmented and doubly diminished intervals have been omitted from the examples, since they're rarely seen.

In case you were wondering, there's no such thing as a diminished unison. Once in a great while, though, you'll run into a doubly augmented or doubly diminished interval. For instance, the interval from C♯ up to B♭ is a diminished 7th, so the interval C♯-B♭♭ would be a doubly diminished 7th. Double flats (♭♭) and double sharps (𝄪) are sometimes needed when notating music in keys that have lots of flats or sharps in their key signature. The rules for when and how to use them are discussed in the section "Chromatic Spelling" in Chapter Seven.

Calling the interval C♯-E♭ a diminished 3rd may seem needlessly academic and fussy. The interval consists of two half-steps — why not just call it a major 2nd? Well, you can call it that if you like. In the real world, it may not make a lot of practical difference. You'll still be able to communicate your ideas to other musicians. But later in this book, we'll see many chords that contain augmented and diminished intervals. An F7♯5 chord, for instance, contains both C♯ and E♭. Calling the interval a major 2nd would obscure the structure of the chord, for reasons that will be explained in Chapter Five. By learning the correct interval names, you'll build a solid foundation for more advanced concepts.

## STACKING INTERVALS

Already in this book you've seen a number of references to stacking intervals — placing one on top of another. The concept is simple, but a clear explanation won't hurt. When two intervals are stacked, the top note of the lower interval is the same as the bottom note of the upper interval. A few examples of stacked intervals are shown in Figure 2-8.

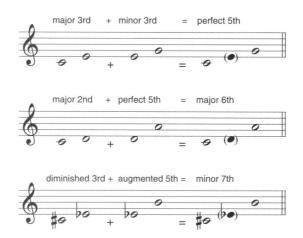

Figure 2-8. Two intervals can be stacked by using the upper note of the first interval as the lower note of the second interval.

As an exercise, you might want to choose a relatively large interval, such as a 5th or 6th, and work out which combinations of smaller intervals can be stacked to produce the larger interval. I've done this with the minor 6th in Figure 2-9. It's easy to do: Simply play the large interval on the keyboard, play any note between the two notes of the interval, and observe the intervals that this inner note forms with the outer two notes. In this case you're splitting an interval rather than stacking two intervals, but the results are the same.

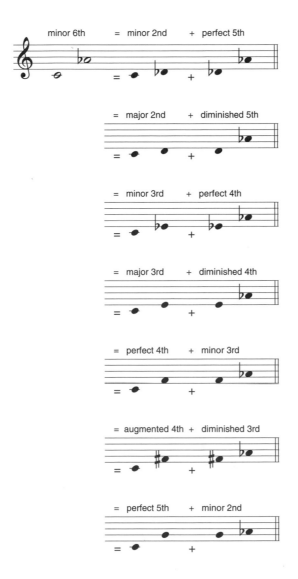

Figure 2-9. Any interval larger than a minor 2nd can be analyzed as two stacked intervals. Here are the primary ways of producing a minor 6th by stacking intervals. (Options such as C-D♯-A♭, which contain doubly diminished or doubly augmented intervals, have been omitted.)

## INVERTED INTERVALS

Generally, it's convenient to talk about intervals by stating the lower note first. When I refer to the interval C-G, for instance, you can safely assume that the C is below the G. But what about the interval G-C? Although the C is an octave higher than before, G-C contains the same two notes as C-G. But as Figure 2-10 makes clear, C-G is a perfect 5th, while G-C is a perfect 4th.

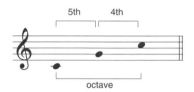

*Figure 2-10. The interval C-G is not the same as the interval G-C.*

These two intervals have a special relationship: The perfect 4th is called an *inversion* of the perfect 5th, and vice-versa. Another way to say this is that if we *invert* a perfect 5th by moving the lower note up an octave, we get a perfect 4th. We'll return to the subject of inversions in Chapter Three. In general, moving the bottom note of a chord or interval up by an octave (or, if necessary, two octaves) so that it's at the top produces an inversion. Likewise, moving the top note down by one or more octaves so that it's at the bottom inverts the chord or interval.

Any pair of intervals that, when stacked, produce a perfect octave are inversions of one another. When two intervals have this relationship, we can also say they're *complementary* or *reciprocal* with respect to one another. The most important pairs of reciprocal intervals are shown in Figure 2-11. As you study this figure, you'll notice that inverting a minor interval always produces a major interval, and vice-versa. Inverting an augmented interval produces a diminished interval, and vice-versa. Inverting a perfect interval produces another perfect interval.

The pairing of reciprocal intervals is important because inverting an interval leaves its harmonic identity and harmonic function intact. In other words, it sounds pretty much the same as it did before. You can verify this at the keyboard. Play the interval C-E, preferably by striking both notes at the same time. Then raise the C by an octave and play E-C in the same manner. Notice how similar the two intervals sound. In many situations, you can invert an interval in this way without changing the harmonic meaning of the passage. The sound will be slightly different, but the harmonic function of the chord that contains the interval will most often be exactly the same. (Figure 6-11 in Chapter Six provides a couple of examples of chords to which this rule doesn't apply.)

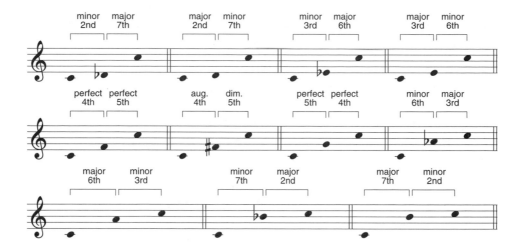

*Figure 2-11. When two intervals can be stacked to form a perfect octave, we say that each interval is the inversion of the other.*

## SOUND COLORS

Each interval has a distinctive sound. And because music can express emotions, it's possible to describe the sounds of intervals in words. While there's not a complete consensus among listeners, many people would subscribe to some or all of the following descriptions:

| | |
|---|---|
| minor 2nd | harsh, biting |
| major 2nd | solid, aggressive |
| minor 3rd | sad, wistful |
| major 3rd | happy, bright |
| perfect 4th | open, somewhat unsettled |
| tritone | alien, very unsettled |
| perfect 5th | open (hollow), solid |
| minor 6th | romantic, plaintive |
| major 6th | uplifting, joyous |
| minor 7th | ominous |
| major 7th | piercing |
| octave | stable or settled, but empty |

In classical music theory, intervals are also classified as *consonant* or *dissonant*. A dissonant interval is one that is harsh-sounding or unsettled. A consonant interval is felt to be solid and stable. The classification of intervals as consonant or dissonant has changed over the centuries, however. In the Medieval and Renaissance periods, it was felt that the only consonant intervals were the unison, perfect 5th, and octave. Major and minor 3rds and 6ths were felt to be dissonant. Music from this period is full of 3rds and 6ths, but the final cadence (the end of the piece) typically ends with a chord consisting only of octaves and perfect 5ths, because composers felt that this ending was necessary in order to resolve the dissonances into consonances.

In the Baroque and Classical periods (roughly 1600-1820), listeners became comfortable accepting the major 3rd as a consonance, but the minor 3rd was still felt to be somewhat dissonant. As a result, pieces written in minor keys often ended in a major key, so that the 3rd of the final chord would be major, not minor. By the Romantic period (1820-1920), ending a piece with a minor chord had become more acceptable.

Due to harmonic developments in the 20th century, including both jazz and atonal classical music, the old distinction between consonant and dissonant intervals has largely evaporated. The only intervals that are still felt as dissonant by most listeners are the minor 2nd, the minor 9th, and, to a lesser extent, the major 2nd. The tritone, which was so disturbing to Renaissance musicians that they called it *diabolus in musica* (the Devil in music) is a consonant interval in jazz: Many jazz songs use a dominant 7th chord, which includes the tritone as the 3rd and 7th of the chord, as the tonic. And the major 7th is the characteristic interval in a major 7th chord, which is used as the tonic in just about all sweet-sounding jazz ballads. (For a full explanation of the intervals in these chords, see Chapter Five.)

In general, musical dissonances *resolve* into consonances. That is, one or more of the voices in a dissonant chord moves upward or downward, usually by a whole-step or half-step, to create a new chord that is consonant. The dissonant chord adds tension to the music, and the resolution of the dissonance into a consonance provides a release of the tension. It's not the case that all chord-based music includes dissonances, or that all dissonances resolve into consonances, but the resolution of dissonance into consonance is certainly central to the language of harmony.

Since we haven't yet explained what makes a chord dissonant, providing an example at this stage is difficult — but not impossible. Figure 2-12, which you may recognize, shows a dissonant interval (a major 2nd) resolving to a consonant interval (a minor 3rd). The resolution is produced by moving one of the notes of the dissonant interval down by a half-step.

*Figure 2-12. The dissonant interval in bar 1 (a major 2nd) resolves to a consonant interval (a minor 3rd) in bar 2.*

## HOW TO HEAR INTERVALS

Learning to discriminate between the sounds of intervals takes practice. Fortunately, there are some mnemonic aids that will make it a little easier.

First, if you're hearing an interval in which both notes are being sounded at the same time, you may find it helpful to mentally break it up into a melodic interval. Imagine that you're hearing the lower note first, followed by the upper note. While practicing this technique, you may want to sing the two notes out loud. Listen to make sure your first note matches the lower note of the interval, and that your second note matches the upper note. Try singing the two notes in the other order, with the upper note first. Be careful not to transpose either of the notes up or down an octave, as this would invert the interval. Depending on your vocal range and where the interval is played, you might have to transpose them *both* up or down. If so, be careful to transpose them both by the same number of octaves.

To figure out what interval you're hearing, you may also find it useful to refer mentally to well-known melodies from pop and classical music. Due to copyright restrictions, it's not possible for us to publish even short excerpts from certain of the tunes listed on the next page. If you can't find them in sheet music form, doubtless a musically knowledgeable friend will be able to play any of the melodies that you don't already know, so that you can hear and become familiar with the intervals. Some of the tunes listed are in the public domain, which means we could publish them here, but a sketchy set of examples in which some of the more useful melodies are omitted would look pretty silly.

You may be able to think of other songs besides the ones listed. Note that some of these tunes use the *ascending* version of the interval (the lower note before the upper one), while others use the *descending* version (upper note first).

| | |
|---|---|
| minor 2nd | Mozart's Symphony No. 40 in G minor (first movement), "Smoke Gets In Your Eyes" |
| major 2nd | "Yesterday," "Silent Night" |
| minor 3rd | "Jingle Bells" (chorus), "America the Beautiful" |
| major 3rd | Beethoven's Symphony No. 5 in C minor (first movement), "When the Saints Go Marchin' In" |
| perfect 4th | "Here Comes the Bride" |
| tritone | "Maria" (from *West Side Story*) |
| major 6th | "Jingle Bells" (verse), "It Came upon a Midnight Clear" |
| octave | "Over the Rainbow," "When You Wish upon a Star" |

## QUIZ

1. What is the name of the interval created by removing one half-step from a perfect 4th? Give two answers — one for the interval in which the letter-names of the two notes have not changed, and another for the interval in which one of the two notes has a new letter-name.
2. When two intervals can be stacked to form a perfect octave, what is their relationship called?
3. If a minor 2nd is increased by an octave, what interval results?
4. How many half-steps are there in a diminished 7th? In a diminished 3rd?
5. Give three different names for the interval that contains six half-steps.
6. Explain why there's no such interval as a perfect 3rd, and no such interval as a minor 5th.
7. Which is larger — a major interval or a minor interval? (Assume that each is spelled with the same two letter-names, so that each has the same number of scale steps.)
8. What note is a major 6th above A? A minor 3rd below G? A diminished 5th below B?
9. What interval is the inversion of a major 3rd? Of a minor 2nd? Of an augmented 4th?
10. What is the name of the interval between the D below Middle C and the D♯ above Middle C?

# 3

# TRIADS

With some exceptions in the area of contemporary classical music, all harmonic activity in conventional European/American music is based on the *triad*. As its name implies, a triad is a set of three notes. Not just any three notes will do, however. The notes in a triad have specific relationships to one another. (In Chapter Six we'll look at a few three-note chords that are not triads.)

A triad is built by stacking two 3rds. As Figure 3-1 shows, there are four ways to do this. We can put a major 3rd on the bottom and a minor 3rd on the top, reverse the order and put a minor 3rd on the bottom and a major 3rd on the top, or combine either two major 3rds or two minor 3rds.

These four triads have names. The first two, which are used somewhat more often, are named after the *lower* of the 3rds: The triad in which the major 3rd is on the bottom and the minor 3rd on top is referred to as a *major triad*. When the minor 3rd is on the bottom and the major 3rd on top, the triad is a *minor triad*.

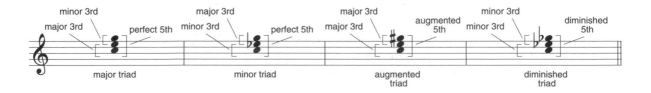

*Figure 3-1. Triads are created by stacking pairs of 3rds. Since each 3rd can be either major or minor, there are four possible triads.*

*Figure 3-2. The names of the notes within a triad.*

The other two types are named after the type of 5th that lies between the bottom and top notes: The triad built out of two major 3rds is called an *augmented triad*, because its outer two notes form an augmented 5th, and the triad built of two minor 3rds is called a *diminished triad*, because its outer two notes form a diminished 5th.

Each of the notes in a triad has a name, as shown in Figure 3-2. The bottom note is called the root, because it's the foundation on which the rest of the triad is built. The middle note is called the 3rd, because the interval between it and the root is a 3rd. The top note is called the 5th, again because the interval between it and the root is a 5th. When we study more complex chords, you'll find that this naming convention is used consistently: Each note in a chord is named after the interval created by its relationship with the root. But as mentioned in Chapter Two, it's important to understand that at this point we're using the terms "3rd" and "5th" in two distinct ways. Any two notes that are the right distance apart form an interval of a 3rd — but the upper note of the interval isn't necessarily the 3rd of the triad in which the two notes are being played. Looking at Figure 3-1, for instance, we can see that the interval of a 3rd separates the E and G in a C major triad. But that doesn't make the G the 3rd of the triad. The G is the 5th of the C major triad, because it's a 5th above the root. (G is also the 3rd of a different triad, one whose root is E.)

## THE DIATONIC TRIADS IN THE MAJOR SCALE

In Chapter Two we looked at all of the intervals that are found in the major scale. We can construct whole triads out of the same scale, as Figure 3-3 shows. Play this example on the keyboard in order to get its sound firmly in your ear. You'll note that major triads are formed on the tonal steps of the scale (the tonic, 4th, and 5th), while the triads built on the modal steps are minor or diminished. There are no augmented triads within the major scale.

These triads are called *diatonic* because they use only the notes of the major scale, with no accidentals. If there were any accidentals in Figure 3-3, we'd have to say that some of the triads were *chromatically altered*. For comparison, play the

*Figure 3-3. The diatonic triads in C major.*

triads in Figure 3-4. The roots of the triads in this figure are all within the major scale, but all of the triads are major.

The only diminished diatonic triad is the one built on the 7th step of the scale. While the other diatonic triads are often used in unaltered form in musical compositions, this diminished triad is rarely used by itself. As you'll learn in the next chapter, however, it's an important part of a more advanced type of chord called a dominant 7th chord.

*Figure 3-4. In order to build a major triad on each step of the C major scale, we have to add accidentals. The first and last chords in each measure are diatonic, because all of their notes are drawn from the C major scale. However, the second and third chords in each measure are chromatically altered: They contain one or more notes that are not part of the C major scale.*

## CHORD NAMES OF TRIADS

Look again at Figure 3-3, and identify the root of each triad. (It's the bottom note in the triad.) The chord name of a triad consists of the letter-name of the root followed by a description of the type of triad. The root of the first triad is C, and it's a major triad, so it's called a C major chord. The root of the second triad is D, and it's a minor triad, so it's a D minor chord. And so on.

In the case of triadic chords — chords that consist of triad notes with no other notes — the word "chord" is often used in place of "triad." If someone refers to a G major chord, for instance, without giving any further description, you can safely assume that they're referring to a triad, a chord containing only the notes G, B, and D.

With this extremely practical bit of knowledge at your fingertips, you'll be able to pick out accompaniments for dozens of well-known songs. Any song that uses only simple triads can be *harmonized* (that is, a harmony part can be added) by playing the appropriate triads beneath the melody. On the keyboard, the usual way to do this is by playing the chords with the left hand and the melody with the right. On the guitar, you'd be more likely to play the chords while singing the melody, though guitar arrangements in which the melody is played on the upper strings while the harmony is filled in on the lower strings are very common. Most guitarists don't play simple triads, however. Chords played on guitar are typically rearranged in various ways. The methods used for rearranging the notes of triads are discussed in the remainder of this chapter, and you'll find some basic information on guitar chord voicings in Appendix B.

In published sheet music, the names of the chords (which might be either simple triads or other chord types) are often placed above or below the melody. Three examples are shown in Figure 3-5. This type of music is called a *lead sheet*, because it contains the lead part (the melody) and is usually printed on a single sheet of paper. In performing the songs in Figure 3-5 on the keyboard, you might play something like the music in Figure 3-6. The left-hand parts in Figure 3-6 show the simplest possible interpretations of the chord symbols in Figure 3-5.

Figure 3-5. Three classic melodies in lead sheet form. The chords to be used for accompaniment are shown. Each chord should be used starting on the beat where the symbol is placed, and should continue until the point in the music where the next chord symbol appears.

The rules for interpreting chord symbols can get a little convoluted, as we'll see in Chapters Five and Six. Fortunately, the basics are unambiguous and easy to remember. When you see a letter-name with no other symbols, play a major chord (one containing only the notes in the major triad). When you see a letter-name followed by the letter "m," play a minor chord (triad). The abbreviations "aug" and "dim" are used for augmented and diminished chords respectively. Some arrangers use a plus sign (+) in place of "aug," a minus sign (–) to indicate a minor chord, and a small raised circle (°) to indicate a diminished chord.

*Figure 3-6. A simple way of performing the songs shown in Figure 3-5. The left-hand parts shown are realizations of the chord symbols in Figure 3-5. Note that some chords are repeated in order to provide a steady rhythm, even though the lead sheet melodies don't show a repetition of the chord symbol. Many of the notes in the melodies are also found in the triads, but a few are not. These non-chord notes are discussed in Chapter Seven, in the section "Non-Chord Tones."*

If you see any chord symbols on the lead sheet other than the letter-name and the abbreviation "m," "aug," or "dim" (or equivalent symbols), the chord has other notes in it besides the notes in the basic triad. Such chords are discussed in Chapters Five and Six.

## INVERSIONS OF TRIADS

The left-hand accompaniment parts in Figure 3-6 look and sound quite stiff, because the chords have been played in the most basic possible way. In order to loosen up the accompaniment, we need to explore some ways to change the chord *voicings*. A voicing is simply a way of arranging or rearranging the notes in the chord. Any combination of notes that includes only notes found within a given chord is a voicing of that chord.

The easiest way to change a basic triadic voicing is to move the bottom note up an octave or the top note down an octave. Doing this produces an *inversion*. Inverting a chord is very much like inverting an interval (see Chapter Two). The main difference is that when an interval is inverted, its name changes: An inverted major 3rd becomes a minor 6th, for example. When a chord is inverted, however, its name remains the same. Also, there are three notes in a triad rather than two, so we have more possible inversions.

When the root of the triad is on the bottom, we say that the triad is in *root position*. When the root is moved up an octave so that the lowest note is the 3rd of the triad, the triad is in *first inversion*. When the 3rd is also moved up, so that the 5th is the lowest note, the triad is in *second inversion*. Figure 3-7 shows these voicings.

When an augmented triad is inverted, something odd and interesting happens: It's not possible to tell that it's inverted by listening to it. For instance, if we invert a Caug triad, as shown in Figure 3-8, we get something that sounds exactly like an Eaug triad. This happens because each major 3rd in an augmented triad is four half-steps wide. There are 12 half-steps in the octave, and 12 divided by four is exactly three, so the augmented triad divides the octave into three equal intervals, each consisting of four half-steps.

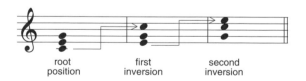

root
position

first
inversion

second
inversion

*Figure 3-7. A C major chord in root position, first inversion, and second inversion. The inversions are created by moving the lowest note up an octave. Although the lowest note in the second chord is E and the lowest note in the third chord is G, these are both still C major chords.*

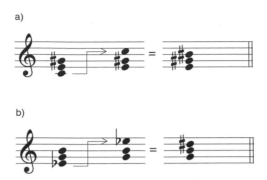

Figure 3-8. *Inverting an augmented triad produces a chord that sounds exactly the same as a different root-position augmented triad. When the C in example (a) is moved up an octave, the voicing contains a stacked augmented 3rd (E-G♯) and diminished 4th (G♯-C). The upper C, however, is enharmonically equivalent to the B♯ in an E augmented triad. The same thing happens in example (b): Inverting the E♭ augmented triad produces the enharmonic equivalent of a G augmented triad.*

The corollary to this is the fact that there are only four different augmented triads on the keyboard, not 12. The notes in the chords Caug, Eaug, and G♯aug (or A♭aug) are identical. The same is true for the three other sets of augmented triads. Here's the complete list of possibilities:

Caug = Eaug = G♯aug

D♭aug = Faug = Aaug

Daug = F♯aug = B♭aug

E♭aug = Gaug = Baug

You can verify this for yourself by locating these triads on the keyboard and listening to the close similarity in their sounds.

## OPEN & CLOSED VOICINGS

Instead of moving the bottom note of the chord up an octave, we can create a new voicing by moving one of the other notes up an octave — or by moving the bottom note down an octave. When we do this, there will be gaps in the chord voicing, as Figure 3-9 shows. Up to now, all of the triads we've looked at have been in *closed position*. This term (many music theorists prefer "close position") is a way of saying that the notes in the chord are as close together as they can get. The second chord in Figure 3-9, however, is in *open position*. In an open-position chord voicing, there are gaps into which other notes belonging to the chord could be inserted.

A triad can be played in a number of different open-position voicings. Figure 3-10 gives some examples. In each case, the lowest note of the voicing defines

*Figure 3-9. A closed-position C major voicing (left) can be turned into an open-position voicing (right) by moving a note other than the lowest note up an octave. In an open-position voicing, there are gaps where other notes belonging to the chord could be played. The gaps are shown here by noteheads in parentheses.*

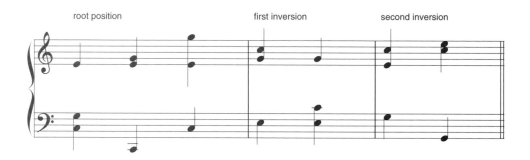

*Figure 3-10. An assortment of open-position voicings of a C major chord.*

the inversion. If the lowest note is the 3rd of the chord, the voicing is in first inversion; if the lowest note is the 5th of the chord, the voicing is in second inversion; and if the lowest note is the root, the voicing is in root position.

There are no names that I'm aware of for the various open-position voicings, but there is one loose rule that you might want to be aware of for forming these voicings. A gap of more than an octave between the lowest note (the bass voice) and the rest of the voicing is common, but chord voicings tend to feel disjointed or unstable if there are gaps wider than an octave between any of the upper notes. The third root-position voicing in Figure 3-10 violates this principle, but to my ears it sounds balanced, so I wouldn't hesitate to use it. Voicings like those in Figure 3-11, however, sound muddy, and most arrangers will avoid them except when they want a special effect.

As you might infer from what I've just said, revoicing a chord changes its sound quality – sometimes subtly, sometimes drastically. A vital aspect of learning to use chords is learning how the various voicings of a given chord sound. This is a concept you should play with, using your favorite chording instrument, as we explore more complex chords in later chapters. Don't just try the voicings shown: Revoice the chords in various ways.

*Figure 3-11. Chord voicings like these, in which two lower voices are in closed position while there's a gap wider than an octave between upper voices, don't tend to sound good.*

## DOUBLED NOTES & DROPPED NOTES

Up to now we've been looking at voicings consisting of only three notes — one each of the notes in the triad. We can vastly increase our palette of available voicings by *doubling* selected notes in higher or lower octaves. When it comes to voicings with doubled notes, the only limits are the number of fingers you have available and/or the range of the instrument(s) you're playing. A few useful voicings that employ doubled notes are shown in Figure 3-12. Try out some other possibilities for yourself while sitting at a keyboard.

When choosing which notes to double, you'll probably find that a voicing with several 3rds but only one root and 5th sounds unstable, if not downright unpleasant. The converse is not necessarily true, however. A voicing with only one 3rd and a couple of roots and 5ths will probably sound okay, though it depends on exactly how the notes lie in relation to one another.

Chord voicings will also sound more pleasant or unpleasant, more stable or unstable, depending on how loud various notes within the voicing are in relation to one another. Good pianists will often strike certain keys harder in order to bring out notes within a chord. In a multi-instrument ensemble, the tone colors of the various instruments playing the notes will also affect the desirability of the voicing for a particular musical passage. Pursuing these topics, however, would take us into the realms of instrumental performance and arranging, which are beyond the scope of this book.

*Figure 3-12. Some good-sounding voicings of a C major chord in which selected notes are doubled in one or more octaves.*

Instead of (or while) doubling certain notes in the chord, we can consider dropping certain notes entirely. Since a triad contains only three distinct notes, doing this will give us a partial, incomplete triad. A partial triad is harmonically ambiguous, as Figure 3-13 demonstrates. In some situations, the ambiguity can be useful: A harmonic ambiguity is a sort of musical pun, because the notes that are played are open to two (or more) different interpretations. In other situations, a partial triad may give the music an unstable or confused sound, which you may not want.

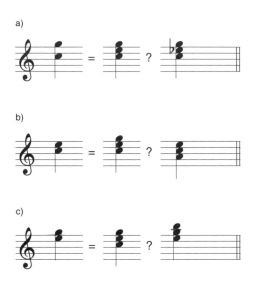

*Figure 3-13. When a note is removed from a triad, the two remaining notes are harmonically ambiguous. Is the two-note voicing in (a) C major or C minor? Is (b) C major or A minor? Is (c) C major or E minor? We may be able to tell by listening to what other instruments are playing at the time, but the chord voicing itself doesn't provide enough information.*

Dropping selected notes from more complex voicings is often appropriate, as explained in Chapter Six, and doesn't necessarily create any harmonic ambiguity (though it may do so).

If you're playing guitar, you may not have as much choice as you'd like about which notes to double, or even what inversion of the chord to use. Accomplished guitarists have various tricks for finding good chord voicings. But when you're just starting out, you'll most likely be playing the standard voicings, some of which are shown in Figure 3-14. Only one of these chords (the E major) is voiced in a balanced way. The C and D chords are in first inversion and the A chord is in second inversion. The G chord has a doubled 3rd and only one 5th.

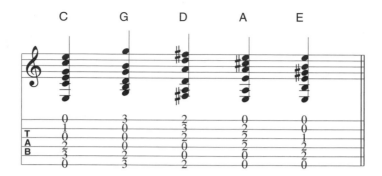

*Figure 3-14. The basic chord fingerings on guitar produce the chord voicings shown here. (The F♯ is often omitted from the low end of the D major chord, because the minor 3rd between the F♯ and the A produces a somewhat muddy sound.) Note that in sheet music written for guitar, the notes are always shown an octave above the pitches that are actually sounded. This makes it easier to write guitar parts in the treble clef. The chords shown here are notated the way a guitar player would read them; if you play the examples on the piano, they'll sound an octave higher than they would on guitar.*

## QUIZ

1. What does the abbreviation "aug" in a chord symbol refer to?
2. Name and play the notes in the following triads: E major, B minor, B♭ major, A augmented, E♭ major, F♯ minor, G diminished, F diminished, D major.
3. Name and play the notes in the following chords: Dm, F, Adim, B, A♭aug, Cm, B♭, D♭, Gaug, E♭m.
4. When the lowest note in a Dm chord voicing is an F, what inversion is the chord in?
5. How many distinct augmented triads are there (considering enharmonic spellings as equivalent)?
6. When a D major chord is played in second inversion, what is the lowest note in the chord voicing?
7. When a D is the lowest note in a B♭ chord, what inversion is the chord in?
8. If a chord symbol contains a letter name and a minus sign, what type of triad would you play?
9. In writing an F minor chord for a five-instrument ensemble, which note or notes would you be most likely to double? Which note or notes would you be least likely to double?
10. Explain the difference between open and closed voicings.

# 4

# CHORD PROGRESSIONS

In the music of some other cultures, it's common for pieces of music to use one chord from start to finish – if, indeed, the music uses structures that are identifiable as chords at all. In music in the European/American tradition, however, pieces that use only one chord are rare. Most pieces make use of at least two or three different chords, which alternate with one another during the course of the piece. Many pieces, even quite short ones, contain upwards of a dozen different chords. By "different," I don't mean different voicings of the same chord, but chords with different roots or of different types.

For the most part, voicings are not shown on lead sheets. Lead sheets will, however, show the types of chords to be used in a piece. They may have different roots, the same root but different 3rds or 5ths (as discussed in Chapter Three), added or altered notes (see Chapters Five and Six), or all of the above.

The order in which the chords occur within the piece is called the *chord progression*. Chord progressions are among the more interesting phenomena in music. To an untrained listener, a melody is the essence of a popular song – but knowledgeable musicians can identify dozens or hundreds of songs merely by hearing the chord progression alone, without the melody. An unusual or provocative chord progression can turn a simple melody into a moving and unforgettable experience, and an unimaginative or clumsy progression can cripple a great melody. Innumerable standard chord progressions are known by millions of musicians, and can be used as the basis for memorable performances in unrehearsed jam sessions.

It's the nature of a piece of music that has a chord progression that the chord being used changes from time to time. Because of this, the chord progression is sometimes called the *chord changes*, or simply "the changes." If someone says to you, "Do you know the changes to 'Satin Doll'?", they're talking about the chord progression of the song.

To complete our definition of the term "chord progression," we need to add one more ingredient. A progression is more than a series of chords that occur in a certain order. The chords almost always fall at specific points within a framework of beats and measures. A full discussion of how music is organized rhythmically would be beyond the scope of this book, but the rest of this chapter will make little sense unless you're familiar with the basics, so a brief detour is in order.

## MEASURES & BEATS

Music is a time-based art. In order to structure time in a way that will allow music to be played, most forms of music divide time into more or less regular beats. The beat is the pulse of the music — and indeed, the beat will often be at about the same rate as a human pulse, or the rate of footsteps in either walking or running.

Beats are grouped into larger units called bars or measures. The terms "bar" and "measure" are synonymous, with one exception: The vertical line between measures in a piece of sheet music is always called a bar line, never a measure line.

The most common groupings place either three or four beats in each measure. For musicians, these groupings become almost second nature: When you're first learning an instrument, you may have to count "*one*-two-three-four" in order to learn the rhythm, emphasizing the first beat of each measure as a way of orienting yourself, but by the time you've been playing for a few years, you should be able to count the beats within a measure without ever thinking consciously about it. (As an aside, counting multi-measure rests seems to be difficult for some musicians. I'm not sure why this should be the case, but I suspect it's because they're relying on their intuitive understanding of beats rather than firing up the rational, mathematical part of the brain.)

Other groupings of beats are sometimes heard. Measures consisting of five or seven beats each are difficult for some musicians to play, but their lively, exciting sound makes it worth the effort to learn how to count and play them. In some music, the number of beats per measure changes from time to time. This compositional technique is especially common in post-19th-century classical music. In pop music, the number of beats per measure will usually remain remain the same throughout a given piece.

Most often, the rhythmic unit that lasts for one beat is the quarter-note. Other note values, such as the eighth-note, half-note, and dotted quarter-note, are sometimes used as the basic unit of the beat, but these are not often used except in classical music.

The grouping of beats into measures is called the *meter*. The word "meter" comes, in fact, from a Greek root that means "measure." The meter of a piece of music is indicated by its *time signature*, which is shown on sheet music as two numbers, one above the other, at the left end of the first staff. The bottom number indicates which note value (quarter-note, eighth-note, etc.) is used for the beat, and the top number shows how many beats are in each measure. Even if these ideas were entirely new to you, from the information above you'd quickly be able to figure out that the most commonly used time signatures are 4/4 (four quarter-notes in each measure) and 3/4 (three quarter-notes in each measure). Some other useful time signatures are shown in Figure 4-1.

Time signatures are generally shown in text with a slash mark (/). However, they're not fractions.

*Figure 4-1. A few of the meters commonly used in popular and classical music. In 6/8, 12/8, and 5/8 time, the time signature indicates that the eighth-note is the rhythmic unit that receives the beat. But in meters that have more than four beats to the bar, the units that receive the beat are generally grouped into units of two or three beats each. In effect, the measure is subdivided into a smaller number of chunks. 6/8 is generally subdivided into two units, each a dotted quarter-note (three eighth-notes) in length. In 12/8, there are four dotted quarter subdivisions. In 5/8 or 5/4 meter, the subdivisions are of unequal length: A bar with five beats is felt as consisting of either three beats followed by two, or two beats followed by three.*

## ASSIGNING CHORDS TO MEASURES & BEATS

In many pieces of music, when the chord that's being used changes, it always does so at the beginning of a new measure — at the bar line. This is more or less the norm, but it's by no means a universal. In some pieces, there are two chords per measure, or even a different chord on every beat. Going the other direction, it's quite common to see pieces in which a single chord lasts for two measures or even longer. Less often, but often enough to be worth knowing about, a new chord begins on the beat before the bar line and continues in the new bar. Quite often, you'll see all of the above in different sections of the same piece.

The timing of the chord changes in a piece is called its *harmonic rhythm*. If there's always a new chord in every bar, the piece has a steady harmonic rhythm. If, on the other hand, a single chord lasts for four measures in the first section of the piece, while in the second section of the same piece a new chord falls on every beat within the bar, the chords change more quickly in the second section, so we'd say the second section has a faster harmonic rhythm.

Using the chord voicing possibilities suggested in Chapter Three, we can begin to construct some simple keyboard parts that follow chord progressions. Figure 4-2 shows one possibility; Figures 4-15 and 4-16 show two others. The progressions shown in Figure 4-3 are a bit more interesting than the one in Figure 4-2, and again they use only triadic chords. We could construct thousands of other examples like these using only the ideas presented so far in this book. After a while they'd all start to sound similar, though. Throwing in a few more complex chords of the types shown later in this book will give a chord progression more spice.

If you play much popular music, sooner or later you're going to find yourself staring at a *chord chart* (see Figure 4-4). A chord chart shows the harmonic rhythm of the music, but neither the chord voicings nor the melody is notated. It's up to the performers to choose appropriate parts to play, using the progression in the chart as a guide. A full discussion of how to construct your own part from a chord chart would be far beyond the scope of this book, but we'll touch on it from time to time. If you're playing bass, you'll usually play the root of each chord in the

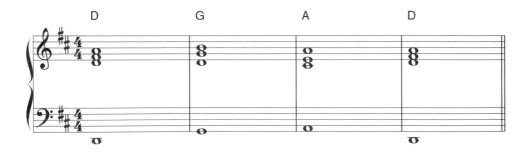

*Figure 4-2. A simple four-bar chord progression.*

indicated rhythm. If you're playing a chording instrument such as guitar or keyboard, you'll more likely play full chord voicings in a rhythm that fits with the style of the music. The bass, guitar, and keyboards can all play from the same chord chart, yet each will play a different part, because the parts to be played are not specified in the chart. Only the bare harmonic skeleton is provided.

Figure 4-3. Three original chord progressions that use only triads. The chord symbols above the treble staff show the progression. As you play or listen to these progressions, try to determine which of the voicings are inversions. Also, analyze the harmonic rhythm. You'll find that some chords last for an entire measure, while other measures contain two, three, or four chords. Note that in (b), the chord voicing sometimes moves even though the underlying chord (as indicated by the chord symbol) isn't changing.

Figure 4-4. A four-bar excerpt from a chord chart. In a chord chart, neither the melody nor the chord voicings is indicated, only the chord types and the harmonic rhythm. Each slash-mark indicates a quarter-note duration. In bar 3 here, a G chord is to be played for two beats, followed by a D chord for two beats.

## CHOOSING CHORDS BY THE NUMBERS

In Chapter Three, I introduced the diatonic triads that are found in a major scale. Not surprisingly, some or all of these triads are used in many or most chord progressions. They're used so often that musicians have developed a shorthand way of referring to them using numbers. Because this system developed some hundreds of years ago, it was usual to use Roman numerals when referring to diatonic triads. (The same numbering system is used by musicians in Nashville, but they no longer use Roman numerals.) The diatonic triads in a given key are referred to as the I, II, III, IV, V, VI, and VII chords, as shown in Figure 4-5.

Some musicians prefer to use lower-case Roman numerals to indicate the minor diatonic triads (ii, iii, and vi). This system is somewhat useful, in that it allows you to indicate quickly the difference between a ii chord (which is minor) and a II (which is major, although it's not a diatonic triad because the 3rd is an altered scale step). However, the upper/lowercase system is not universally employed. If you see the notation II or III, you can't be certain that whoever wrote it meant you to play a major chord.

Occasionally you'll see this numbering system extended to refer to chords whose roots are not in the diatonic scale. A ♭VI chord, for instance, is one whose root is on the lowered 6th degree of the scale (A♭ in the key of C), and so on. This system has an inherent weakness when it comes to verbal communication, however. Some of the chords we'll discuss later in this book include a flatted 5th, and are called "flat-five" (♭5) chords. A ♭5 chord is not the same thing as a ♭V chord. One is a triad with a lowered 5th, and the other is a chord built on the flatted 5th step of the scale. But in most situations, it will be clear from the context which type of chord the speaker is referring to.

The practice of referring to chords by number is very commonly used. Improvising musicians talk routinely about various sorts of II-V progressions, for instance. If a musician says to you, "That's a two-five in the key of B♭," he or she is talking about a progression in which some variety of C chord (the II in the key of B♭) is followed by some variety of F chord (the V in B♭).

We humans have a penchant for giving names to things, so maybe it's not surprising that there's another whole set of terminology that can be used to refer to

*Figure 4-5. The diatonic triads in a given key are often referred to using Roman numerals. Purely for the sake of variety, this example is given in the key of E.*

| tonic | supertonic | mediant | subdominant | dominant | submediant | leading tone |

*Figure 4-6. The scale steps also have names, as shown here for the key of C major.*

the same group of diatonic chords. As Figure 4-6 shows, each note (scale step or chord root) in the major scale has a name. The I note/chord we've already seen referred to as the tonic, but the other terms are new.

The most important terms in Figure 4-6 are "dominant" and "subdominant," for reasons discussed in the next section. The term "leading tone" is also important, but for slightly different reasons. The terms "supertonic," "mediant," and "submediant" are rarely heard outside of music theory classrooms.

The term "leading tone" almost always refers to the single note below the tonic, not to a chord built on that note. This note is called the leading tone because in a V-I progression, the 3rd of the V chord almost always moves upward to the root of the I chord (see Figure 4-7). In the natural minor scale (see Chapter Seven), the note below the tonic is sometimes referred to as the subtonic, because it doesn't tend to move upward to the tonic.

Other than in classical music, chords are seldom built using the leading tone as a root, because the diminished triad is felt to be too unstable. Rock songs often use the major triad built on the lowered VII, however. In classical music, the VII triad sometimes substitutes for a V7 chord (see Chapter Five), because it contains all of the notes of the V7 except the root. In this usage the VII chord is almost always in first or second inversion.

*Figure 4-7. The leading tone (B in the key of C major) gets its name from the fact that in a V-I progression, the leading tone almost always moves upward to the tonic.*

## FIGURED BASS

Musicians in the Baroque period had a system of symbols that could be used for writing out chord charts. Just as jazz players do today, harpsichordists and other instrumentalists would improvise their own parts based on the symbols in the

*Figure 4-8. Baroque musicians used a system called* figured bass *to indicate chord parts. As explained in the text, a "6" below a bass note indicates that the chord is in the first inversion, "6 4" means second inversion, and "2" indicates a 7th chord in third inversion. The bass part shown in (a) might be realized by a harpsichordist in the manner shown in (b).*

chart. This system, which is called *figured bass*, is of very little practical value today unless you happen to be a harpsichord player, but it's worth mentioning, if only because you may encounter it somewhere along the line, such as in a college-level textbook or test.

Figured bass consists of a notated bass line with numbers below certain of the notes, as shown in Figure 4-8. The system of figures, which is sensible enough, if a bit abstract, was later applied by music theorists to the system of indicating chords with Roman numerals. The same numbers that had been used in figured bass were placed to the right of the Roman numeral, thus indicating in a compact way the root of the chord (the Roman numeral), its inversion, and any additional notes contained in the voicing.

A Roman numeral to which figured bass numbers have been attached may have a small superscript number beside it, or in some cases both superscript and subscript numbers. A chord in first inversion has a superscript "6" beside the Roman numeral. This indicates that the interval between the bass note and the root is a 6th. For instance, a III$^6$ chord in the key of D major would be an F♯ minor chord in which the A is in the bass (so that the interval between the bass and the root is a 6th). The basic idea is that in the absence of any numbering, the expected chord will have notes a 3rd and a 5th above the bass, so any deviations from this pattern will be noted.

A chord in second inversion uses both a superscript "6" and a subscript "4" (for instance, I$^6_4$), because the notes above the bass are, respectively, a 6th and a 4th above it, rather than a 5th and 3rd. Chords containing 7ths, which will be introduced in the next chapter, can also be indicated with this system. A root-position 7th chord has a superscript "7" (for instance, $IV^7$). A 7th chord in first inversion has a superscript "6" and a subscript "5." In second inversion, a 7th chord has a superscript "4" and a subscript "3." In third inversion, a 7th chord is indicated with a superscript "4" and a subscript "2," or just a subscript "2" by itself.

Now that you've learned about figured bass, feel free to forget about it. Once in a while you may hear a classically trained musician refer to a first-inversion 7th chord as a 6-5 chord, or to a second-inversion triad as a 6-4 chord, but other than that, the system is pretty much obsolete once you step outside the college classroom.

## THE IMPORTANCE OF THE TONIC

In Chapter One we talked about constructing a major scale starting on any note in the chromatic scale. I showed how key signatures derive their names from the note that's the tonic of the major scale played using that key signature. For instance, the B♭ key signature (which contains two flats, one on B and the other on E) allows us to notate a B♭ major scale without using any accidentals. The tonic of the key is important not just for defining the starting point of the scale, but because the triad built on the tonic chord — that is, the I chord — provides an important point of reference in any chord progression in that key.

In the discussion that follows, I'll use the word "tonic" to refer not to the root note of the key but to the entire triad (or, potentially, a more complex chord) built on that root. The same type of usage is used for the dominant and subdominant: These words more often refer to whole chords than to scale steps.

The tonic is a sort of anchor or resting point. Many songs — perhaps a majority — use chord progressions that both begin and end on the tonic. And when chords other than the tonic are used, they're often part of a progression that is moving either toward the tonic or away from it.

This fact opens up some interesting compositional possibilities. A composer can add tension to a chord progression by violating our expectations with respect to the tonic. For instance, a piece might *not* begin on the tonic. As a young man, Beethoven served notice to the audiences in Vienna that he was a force to be reckoned with by beginning his *First Symphony* not on the tonic but on a somewhat distant chord. In the pop realm, the jazz standard "Autumn Leaves" uses the same technique.

Next to the tonic, the most important diatonic chord is the dominant — the V chord. From the 18th century onwards, the chord progression V-I — a dominant followed by a tonic — has been the most important progression in European/American music. This progression strongly emphasizes the tonic as a point of rest. Consequently, the dominant chord is felt to provide a kind of tension that demands resolution through movement to a tonic. Many classical symphonies in the late 18th and early 19th centuries ended with a string of dominant-tonic progressions; a typical example is shown in Figure 4-9. This type of ending hammered home the tonic as the final resting point in the piece.

Next in importance to the dominant and tonic is the subdominant. Looking at Figure 4-9, you might think this note/chord gets its name from the fact that it's the scale step below the dominant ("sub-" is a Latin prefix that means "below"). But in fact the name is derived from the fact that the dominant is a 5th above the tonic, while the subdominant is a 5th *below* the tonic.

*Figure 4-9. The dominant-tonic (V-I) progression is the most important progression in the classical music of the late 18th and early 19th centuries. The progression shown here, which alternates V and I chords in the key of C, illustrates how a symphony written in this period might come to its thrilling conclusion.*

In music of the late 18th and early 19th centuries (the so-called Classical period in classical music), the subdominant was often deployed just before the dominant in a progression leading back to the tonic. This IV-V-I progression is shown in Figure 4-10. This progression is still used in many modern pop tunes, especially in country and folk music, which tend to use relatively simple changes. In jazz and jazz-derived styles, however, the IV has been largely supplanted by the minor II chord, also shown in Figure 4-10. If you play these progressions, you should be able to hear that the IV chord (the subdominant) and the minor II chord are similar in sound, and perform a similar harmonic function. The minor II chord in first inversion was often used in place of the IV chord in Classical progressions as well.

*Figure 4-10. The IV-V-I progression, used in traditional classical music, and the II-V-I progression, used more often in jazz, are similar.*

## PHRASES & CADENCES

It's useful to look at a piece of music of any significant length not as a single seamless entity, but as a series of *phrases*. The end of each phrase flows into the beginning of the next, usually without a pause. The most common lengths for phrases are four and eight bars, but odd-length phrases, such as five or ten bars, are by no means unusual.

The division of a longer piece into phrases usually feels very natural. As you listen to music, you'll probably be able to identify phrases without trouble. If you're in doubt, when looking at sheet music, about where one phrase ends and the next begins, try counting out groups of four or eight bars. Chances are, you'll be able to find the phrases this way.

The portion of a chord progression that ends a phrase is called a *cadence*. As you can probably anticipate from the section above on "The Importance of the Tonic," many cadences end on the I chord. A cadence in which the I is preceded by a V (for an example, see Figure 4-9) is called a *full cadence* or an *authentic cadence*. But not all cadences are full cadences. For that matter, not all V-I progressions are cadences. A cadence is specifically what happens at the end of a phrase.

If the last chord in the phrase is a V chord, the cadence is called a *half cadence*. Figure 4-11 shows a simple progression in the key of G in which the first four-bar phrase ends on a half cadence on D (the dominant of G) and the second four-bar phrase on a full cadence. A cadence in which the I is preceded by a IV rather than a V, as in the "Amen" that ends many hymns, is called a *plagal cadence*.

If all V chords were followed by I chords, the world would be a dull place. Composers often trick their listeners by leading up to a V chord and then following it with something *other* than a I chord. This is called a *deceptive cadence*. The

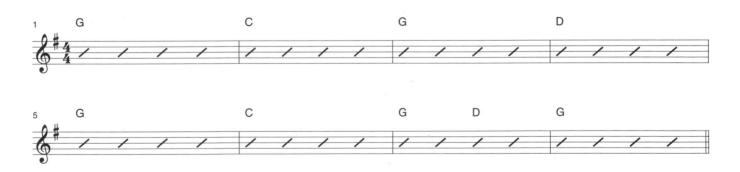

*Figure 4-11. This eight-bar progression, used in many country and bluegrass tunes, consists of two four-bar phrases. The first phrase ends on the dominant (D in the key of G), making it a half cadence. The second phrase ends with a V-I progression. Because the last chord in the phrase is a I, the phrase ends with a full cadence.*

chord most often substituted for the I in a deceptive cadence is the VI (see Figure 4-12). One reason the VI is often chosen is because the VI and the I share two notes (the tonic and mediant), which makes the substitution sound natural. Another reason is because the VI is a minor triad, whose piquant sound adds meaning to the deceptive cadence. Other chords can be used in deceptive cadences, as Figure 4-12 suggests.

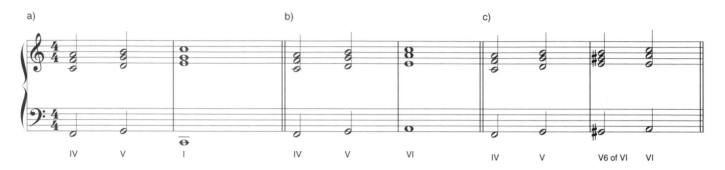

Figure 4-12. In a deceptive cadence, a I chord is expected, as in (a), but instead a different chord is substituted for the I, most often a minor VI. A deceptive cadence using the minor VI is shown in (b). The deceptive cadence in (c) uses a technique we'll look at more closely in Chapter Five: The E major triad is not part of the key of C major, but instead is a secondary dominant leading to the A minor triad. In other words, although this progression is in C major, it contains a V-I progression in the key of A minor.

## MAJOR & MINOR KEYS

Up to now, we've been talking about major scales and mostly using progressions in major keys as examples. Many pieces of music are written, however, in which a minor chord is used as the tonic. Such pieces are said to be in a minor key.

Each of the 12 key signatures can be used either for a major key or for the minor key that uses (mostly) the same set of accidentals. The minor key in this case is the one whose scale starts on the VI of the major scale. For instance, A minor corresponds to C major (because A is the VI in the key of C major), D minor corresponds to F major, and so on. The key of A minor is said to be the relative minor of the key of C major. In the same way, E minor is the relative minor of G major, F♯ minor the relative minor of A major, and so on.

We can use the same terminology when referring to notes and chords in a minor key that we would use in a major. Figure 4-13 shows how the basic terms would be applied to the key of A minor. As you play this example, you should notice one or two important things. First, because the diatonic triads in A minor are exactly the same as those in C major, it's a little difficult to tell, simply by listening, which key you're in. Your ear may tend to drift back toward hearing the music in C major, because the major scale exerts a kind of magnetic pull. Second, the dominant and subdominant triads in the minor key are minor triads. Because of this, the dominant-tonic progression in particular isn't very forceful.

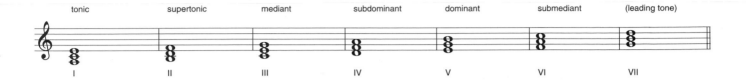

| tonic | supertonic | mediant | subdominant | dominant | submediant | (leading tone) |
|---|---|---|---|---|---|---|
| I | II | III | IV | V | VI | VII |

Figure 4-13. Diatonic triads in the key of A minor. As noted in the text, the term "leading tone" is usually used to refer to the note below the tonic, not to an entire triad built on that note.

The solution to both of these difficulties, which has been commonly used by composers since before the time of Bach, is to alter the 3rd of the dominant when the music is in a minor key. In the key of A minor, more often than not a composer will use an E major chord as the dominant. Once in a while, the subdominant may also have a raised 3rd, but most often this harmony is the result of voice-leading considerations. An altered dominant in A minor is shown in Figure 4-14.

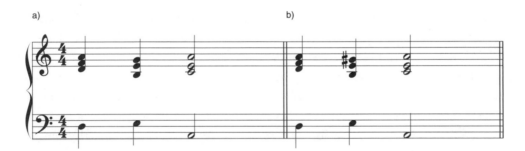

Figure 4-14. Two IV-V-I progressions in A minor. In (a), the V chord is strictly diatonic; it uses the G♮ in the key signature. In (b), the V chord has been altered to E major, providing a G♯ leading tone. This provides a much stronger cadence.

At this point, however, our harmonic system has developed a new ambiguity. Looking again at Figure 4-13, what happens to the III chord if we sharp the 3rd of the V chord? In place of a C major III in A minor, we suddenly have a Caug III. This may or may not be desirable at any given spot in the chord progression.

In practice, composers deal with this ambiguity by freely altering the 6th and 7th steps of the minor scale, or not doing so, based on what's needed at the moment. Both the 6th and 7th steps of the minor scale are heard in two different versions, altered or unaltered, sometimes within the same measure. Most often, the 7th step is raised to form a leading tone for harmonic reasons — that is, to provide a major dominant triad — while the 6th step is raised for melodic reasons in a line that is moving upward from the 5th to the 7th. The inherent instability of the 6th and 7th steps of the minor scale gives music in minor keys a kind of chromatic richness not found in the major keys. This fact, in combination with the darker color of the minor I chord itself, is what causes music written in minor keys to be more emotion-laden or plaintive than similar music written in a major key.

When we turn our attention, in Chapter Seven, to scales, we'll take a closer look at the variations in the minor scale.

As noted above, the relative minor of a major key has its root on the 6th step of the major scale. To look at it another way, the tonic of the relative minor is a minor 3rd below the tonic of the major. Each major key also has a *parallel minor* key. The tonic of the parallel minor is the same as the tonic of the major. G minor, for instance, is the parallel minor of G major.

## OTHER DIATONIC PROGRESSIONS

Even with the limited resources provided by diatonic triads, we can create a number of usable, interesting progressions. One possible example is shown in Figure 4-15. Also, many rock songs use progressions that involve only diatonic triads. Whole songs have been written using nothing but an endlessly repeated I-IV-I-IV progression. And you probably learned to play the music in Figure 4-16 (a I-VI-IV-V progression) when you were eight or nine years old.

This figure illustrates an important property of chord progressions, especially as they're used in pop music. Some progressions have a natural tendency to repeat. The end of the progression tends to lead the ear back to the beginning. A repeating progression — or, for that matter, a repeating bass line, rhythm, or melody — is called a *riff*. The word can also be used as a verb: "Then you riff on the I-VI for 32 bars."

*Figure 4-15. A simple but musical progression that uses only diatonic chords.*

Swing eighths

*Figure 4-16. A familiar diatonic progression that repeats. Rather than stick with boring block chords, I've notated this example using a bouncy rhythm. From time to time, the examples in this book will be given with rhythms. Please feel free to try any of the block chord examples using any rhythm pattern that appeals to you.*

## QUIZ

1. Define the following terms: changes, harmonic rhythm, relative minor, deceptive cadence, riff.
2. What is the diatonic III chord in the key of A major? The V chord in F major? The II chord in B minor? In each case, identify the type of triad (major, minor, augmented, or diminished).
3. What chord follows the dominant in an authentic cadence?
4. Which diatonic triad or triads are most often altered in a minor key? Which note in each triad is altered, and how is it altered?
5. Identify all of the chords in Figure 4-15 as I, II, III, IV, etc. Also, indicate which of the chords are inverted. Which inversions are used?
6. Which of the diatonic triads in the major scale is used least often, and why is it not used?

# 5

# 7TH CHORDS & CHORD SYMBOLS

The first four chapters of this book have been devoted to fundamentals. While the concepts we've covered are essential, they aren't the most inspiring musically. Starting in this chapter, though, we're going to be exploring some ideas that it's possible to actually have fun with. If you work through the material carefully, by the time you reach the end of the chapter you'll have a large and useful repertoire of chord voicings that can be applied in a wide variety of situations.

## STACKING ANOTHER 3RD ON A TRIAD

In Chapter Three, I explained how to build triads, which are the most basic type of chord, by stacking two 3rds on top of one another. As Figure 3-1 on page 41 shows, because we have two 3rds to work with, we can create a total of four different triads.

There's no reason to stop with three notes, however. When we stack another 3rd on top of a triad, we create an immensely useful structure. This new chord — or rather, chord family, since it includes a number of distinct chord types — is known as the 7th chord. It gets its name from the fact that the new note is a 7th above the root (see Figure 5-1).

If you know a little math, you might expect that there would be eight different 7th chords, because we can stack either a major or minor 3rd on top of each of the four triads, and 4 x 2 = 8. However, if we stack three major 3rds, the top note will be an octave (technically, an augmented 7th) above the root, which means we've essentially just built an augmented triad with a doubled root. So

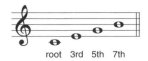

root  3rd  5th  7th

*Figure 5-1. By stacking another 3rd on top of the triad, we can create a useful structure known as a 7th chord.*

there are only seven basic 7th chords. These are shown in Figure 5-2. Some other 7th chords will be covered later in the chapter.

The problem that immediately arises is what to call these chords. The question of chord names is going to get even more convoluted as we explore more complex chords, so you may as well accept the fact that you're going to have to memorize some terms and conventions. What's more, the names used by academic types to describe 7th chords are slightly different from those used by jazz players. In addition, a whole system of abbreviations is used when chords are indicated in chord symbols. The more interesting things get harmonically, the messier the nomenclature will become.

Fortunately, the names of the 7th chords are pretty easy to understand and remember. The academic names are quite systematic: Each chord is named using the type of triad followed by the type of 7th — that is, the type of 7th interval between the root and the 7th of the chord. In a case where the two terms are the same, such as the major-major 7th (major triad with a major 7th, minor triad with a minor 7th, and diminished triad with a diminished 7th), the academic names are shortened. Thus "major 7th chord" really means "major-major 7th chord" and so on.

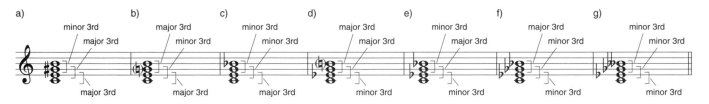

*Figure 5-2. Combining major and minor 3rds in various combinations allows us to create seven different 7th chords.*

**Major 7th.** Looking at the chord in Figure 5-2b, you'll see that it's diatonic in the key of C major. That is, the root of the chord is the same as the tonic of the scale it's drawn from. This makes it easy to remember that the chord is called a major 7th. Note that the name is *not* derived simply from the type of 7th interval that lies between the root and the 7th of the chord: The chords in 5-2a and 5-2d also have major 7ths. The name "major 7th" is reserved exclusively for the chord that has both a major triad and a major 7th.

**Dominant 7th.** Next, look at the chord in Figure 5-2c. This chord is also found in a diatonic scale — but not in the key of C major. It's found in the F major scale. In the key of F, this chord is the *dominant 7th*, so called because its root is the V (the dominant) of the scale. The dominant 7th is arguably the most important of the 7th chords. It's found in practically every piece of music that uses conventional chords, even in styles (such as folk and country) where the other 7th chords are avoided. The dominant 7th chord is built on a major triad, but the 7th interval between the root and 7th is minor, not major. Some academics refer to this chord as the dominant 7th when it's actually a V7 chord, and as a major-minor 7th otherwise.

**Minor 7th.** Another chord in Figure 5-2 is found in major scales, but not with the root of the chord on the tonic of the scale. The *minor 7th* chord (Figure 5-2e) built on C is diatonic in the keys of B♭, A♭, and E♭. You can verify this for yourself by playing each of these scales and picking out the notes of the C minor 7th chord: In the key of B♭, it's the II chord, in A♭ it's the III chord, and in E♭ it's the VI chord. (Note that I'm using the terms "II chord," "III chord," and "VI chord" a bit loosely here. Normally these terms refer only to triads, not to 7th chords. The correct terminology is explained below.) The minor 7th chord gets its name from the fact that both the triad and the 7th are minor.

**Half-Diminished 7th.** There's yet a fourth 7th chord in Figure 5-2 that's diatonic in the major scale. The chord in 5-2f, called a *half-diminished 7th*, is diatonic in the key of D♭ major, where its root is the leading tone (VII). In Chapter Four, I noted that the triad built on the leading tone hasn't been used much since the early 19th century, except in combination with other notes. One of the notes that can turn this triad into a more useful entity is the added 7th. The half-diminished 7th chord is heard quite commonly in jazz arrangements. Unlike the major 7th, minor 7th, and dominant 7th, however, it's a somewhat unstable chord. It almost always functions as a lead-in to some other chord. The half-diminished chord is also referred to as a m7♭5 chord, because it contains a diminished (flatted) 5th.

**Diminished 7th.** The chord in Figure 5-2g, while not used as often in modern music as it was in the 19th century, is one of the more interesting features of the 12-note equal-tempered scale. It consists of three stacked minor 3rds. As a result, the interval between the root and the 7th is a *diminished 7th*. The fact that both the triad and the 7th are diminished gives the chord its name.

What's interesting about the diminished 7th chord is that it's entirely symmetrical: Simply by listening to the chord, it's not possible to tell which of the four notes is the root. Another way to look at it is to say that the diminished 7th chord doesn't really have a root at all. The same four chromatic pitches are found in the C diminished 7th, the E♭ diminished 7th, the G♭ (or F♯) diminished 7th, and the A diminished 7th chords, so which note we call the root is more or less arbitrary.

Depending on the key signature and other factors, however, some of the notes in the diminished 7th may need to be re-spelled using enharmonic equivalents. For instance, Figure 5-2g shows the top note of the C diminished 7th chord as a B♭♭, which is the enharmonic equivalent of A. The spelling will sometimes give a music theorist a clue about which note the composer intended to be the root. On the other hand, jazz musicians often write charts in which diminished 7ths are spelled in the way that's most convenient to read — usually, with the bass note as the root — rather than in the way that's academically correct. The C diminished 7th should technically include a B♭♭, for instance, because this note forms the interval of a diminished 7th with the root. Don't be surprised, though, when you see a C diminished 7th spelled with an A♮ rather than a B♭♭. Technically, a chord consisting of the notes A, C, E♭, and G♭ is an A diminished 7th, because the 7th interval is between A and G♭. But the chord progression might not make much sense if the chord were referred to as an A rather than a C chord. In any case, the chord's ambiguity renders this distinction pretty much irrelevant.

Because each diminished 7th chord is in reality four different diminished 7th chords, there are only three distinct diminished 7th chords in the chromatic scale. To give them their convenient (rather than academically correct) spellings, the three chords are A-C-E♭-F♯, B♭-C♯-E-G, and B-D-F-A♭ (see Figure 5-3).

Figure 5-3. Because the diminished 7th chord is symmetrical with respect to the 12-tone equal-tempered scale, the scale contains only three different diminished 7th chords, which are shown here. Any of the four notes in one of these chords can function as its root. While there's a correct way to choose enharmonic spellings for the notes, in practice most arrangers choose a spelling that's easy to read.


**Augmented-Major 7th & Minor-Major 7th.** The last two 7th chords are used less often than the first five, but they provide distinctive harmonic colors that are worth knowing about. The *augmented-major 7th*, shown in 5-2a, gets its name from the fact that it includes an augmented triad and a major 7th. The *minor-major 7th* (Figure 5-2d) gets its name from the minor triad and major 7th. In both cases, the name mentions the type of triad first, and then the type of 7th.

For review, let's look at the chords in Figure 5-2 again (see Figure 5-4), this time with their names. The major-key diatonic 7th chords are identified in Figure 5-5.

**The Colors of the 7th Chords.** It's difficult or impossible to fully explain the meaning of any type of music or musical phenomenon in words. If it were easy, we wouldn't need music! Nevertheless, as we get deeper into harmony, it becomes

*Figure 5-4. The chords in Figure 5-2 have names, which are shown here. As usual, all of the chords are shown with a C root, purely for convenience. You should try transposing these chords to the other 11 roots in the scale to get a feel for how they appear on the keyboard.*

clear that the chords we're exploring have emotional connotations. That's what makes them useful.

Without wishing to restrict your own usage of these chords or the meaning you find in them, which may be different from anything other musicians have ever envisioned, we can make a couple of basic observations. Most listeners feel that the major 7th chord has a pleasant, settled, happy sound. The minor 7th, in contrast, is more sad and thoughtful. The dominant 7th is bold and purposeful. The major-augmented and minor-major 7ths are edgy and unsettled; because of their instability, they're used most often as transitional chords. The half-diminished 7th is also a transitional chord, but its sound is warmer. The diminished 7th chord is ambiguous and therefore very unstable. It always serves as a lead-in to some other, more stable chord.

*Figure 5-5. The diatonic 7th chords in the major scale.*

## CHORD SYMBOL ABBREVIATIONS

Having to write out the full name of a chord type in sheet music each time the chord is employed would make for a messy, hard-to-read page. Musicians have come up with concise abbreviations for many commonly used chord types — not just 7th chords, but other types, as explained in later chapters. While there is not complete agreement among musicians about which abbreviations should be used to indicate which chords, only a few systems (which are similar to one another except for details) are in common use. These symbols are very commonly employed in lead sheets. In fact, we've already seen a few of them in Chapter Three.

The general rules that are employed for generating basic chord symbols are as follows:

**1.** The root of the chord is indicated by its letter name (almost always shown as a capital letter). Any chord whose root is C will have an abbreviation that begins with the letter C. If necessary, an accidental will be part of the root name. A chord whose root is F♯, for instance, will have an abbreviation that begins with the letter F followed by the sharp sign.

**2.** Numbers in the abbreviation always indicate the notes in extended voicings. All of the basic 7th chords, for instance, use the number 7. Thus if there is no number, a simple triad is indicated.

**3.** Since the 3rd of the chord is so important for giving it a characteristic color and function, the 3rd is indicated immediately following the root — but only if such an indication is needed in order to make the abbreviation clear. A major 3rd is indicated either with the letters "maj" or with a capital "M." A minor 3rd is indicated either with the letters "min" or a lowercase letter "m," or with a minus sign (–). In this book, I'll use "maj" for major and "m" for minor. (I recommend not using a capital "M" for major chords, because many people's handwriting doesn't make a clear enough distinction between "m" and "M." In computer-printed charts, "M" is acceptable, but it's bound to be confusing to use abbreviations in printed music that you wouldn't use in handwritten music.)

**4.** In general, the most commonly used chords have the simplest abbreviations. This makes the chord symbols easier to read. As a result, it's not often necessary to spell out the type of 3rd, 5th, and 7th (or other notes) used in a chord, except with chords that are used less often.

These principles should help you understand why the specific symbols explained below have the form that they do.

**1.** A letter name not followed by any other sign indicates a major triad — for instance, the chord symbol "D" by itself indicates a D major triad, with no 7th or other notes (see Figure 5-6). All other chord symbols have suffixes.

*Figure 5-6. Chord symbols with no suffixes denote major triads. (A flat or sharp in the letter name is not considered a suffix.) Most of the chords in Figures 5-6 through 5-10 are shown in closed position purely for convenience — chord symbols do not show whether a chord is to be voiced in closed or open position.*

**2.** A letter name followed by "m" or "min" indicates a minor triad, again with no 7th. The same holds true for letter names followed simply by "aug" or "dim" — they refer to augmented and diminished triads, respectively (see Figure 5-7). In jazz charts, the diminished triad is indicated even more commonly with a small, raised circle next to the root name, for instance "F°". (This symbol is sometimes used to indicate a diminished 7th chord rather than a simple diminished triad. Since diminished triads are seldom used without other notes, this abbreviated usage makes sense.)

*Figure 5-7. Minor triads are indicated with the suffix "m" (or "min"), augmented triads with the suffix "aug," and diminished triads with the suffix "dim."*

**3.** A letter name followed by a "7" with no other indication indicates a dominant 7th voicing. While there are other 7th chords, the dominant 7th is used somewhat more often than other types, or at any rate is felt to be more basic, so it gets the nod for the simplest abbreviation (see Figure 5-8).

*Figure 5-8. When the suffix of the chord symbol is "7" with no other indication, a dominant 7th chord is meant.*

**4.** The major 7th, minor 7th, and diminished 7th chords are indicated with the suffix "maj7" (or "M7"), "m7" (or "min7"), and "dim7" (or "°7"). With both the maj7 and m7 chords, the "maj" or "m" conveniently tells us how to play both the 3rd and the 7th of the chord (see Figure 5-9). Some arrangers use a triangle after the root letter to indicate a major 7th chord.

*Figure 5-9. The suffix "maj7 (or "M7") indicates a major 7th chord, "m7" (or "min7") indicates a minor 7th chord, and "dim7" (or "°7") indicates a diminished 7th chord.*

**5.** This leaves us with the half-diminished, augmented-major, and minor-major 7th chords. Because these are somewhat less common, they have to make do with the messiest abbreviations (see Figure 5-10). The half-diminished 7th, in fact, has two abbreviations, which are used interchangeably. Some arrangers indicate it with a superscript o, like the diminished 7th, but with a slash through the o, like this: Ø7. It's also known as a "minor seven-flat-five" chord, abbreviated "m7♭5" (or "min7♭5"), because it contains the same 3rd and 7th as the minor 7th chord, together with a lowered (flatted) 5th.

The augmented-major 7th is indicated in a similar way. The 3rd and 7th are the same as those in the maj7 chord, but the 5th is raised, so it's indicated with the suffix "maj7♯5" (or "M7♯5"). The 7th chord with a minor 3rd and major 7th has the clumsiest abbreviation we've seen so far. The suffix used is "m-maj7" (or "min-maj7"), indicating the triad first and then the 7th.

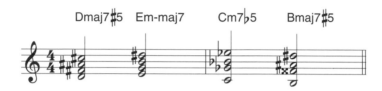

*Figure 5-10. The suffixes "maj7♯5", "m-maj7", and "m7♭5" are used for the chord types shown.*

## INVERTING 7TH CHORDS

Because a 7th chord has four notes, it can be played in four different inversions: in root position or in first, second, or third inversion. The first and second inversions of triads have already been discussed in Chapter Three. When a 7th chord is played in third inversion, the 7th is the lowest note. The basic possibilities are shown in Figure 5-11.

The chord symbol abbreviations shown in Figures 5-6 through 5-10 don't include any information about which inversion to use. In many situations, the choice of inversion is left up to the player — and in fact, if several players are reading from the same chord chart, each may use a different inversion. This is a good thing: It helps listeners hear the chording instruments as distinct entities. What ultimately determines the inversion listeners will hear, in any case, is the note played by the bass player. As a result, chord symbols sometimes include an indication of which note should be played in the bass. This is normally done by adding a slash mark (/) after the chord symbol, and following the slash mark with the name of the bass note. For instance, the chord symbol Cmaj7/B would be a C major 7th chord with the B in the bass — a chord in third inversion.

Some arrangers prefer to use chord symbols with slash marks to indicate that two complete chords are to be played at the same time (a technique known as

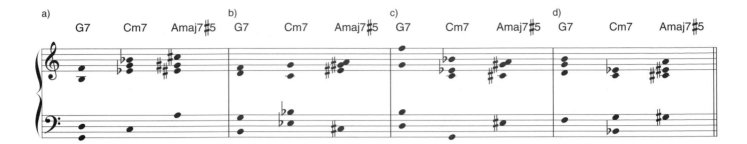

Figure 5-11. Three different 7th chords, each shown in root position (a), first inversion (b), second inversion (c), and third inversion (d). Note that the second and third inversions of the Amaj7#5 chord sound harmonically ambiguous, because of the prominent C# major triad contained within the chord.

*bitonalism*, which will be discussed briefly in Chapter Six). If the arranger is using this approach, single bass notes will be indicated by adding the word "bass" — for example, "Cmaj7/B bass." In general, though, it's fairly safe to assume that a note mentioned after a slash mark is a bass note, not an indication that you're to play a bitonal chord voicing.

In some situations, the bass note named with this type of symbol won't actually be part of the indicated chord. For instance, the arranger may use the symbol "C/B" to indicate a C triad above a B bass note. In this case, the result is a Cmaj7 chord in third inversion, but the chording instruments are more likely to be playing a straight C major triad rather than a Cmaj7 voicing. The bass may be the only instrument playing the B. If chording instruments add a B, they will likely do so in a lower octave rather than at the top of the voicing. The indication "C/B" is both easier to read than "Cmaj7/B" and gives a clearer indication of what the arranger has in mind.

This type of situation is especially common with descending bass line passages like the one shown in Figure 5-12.

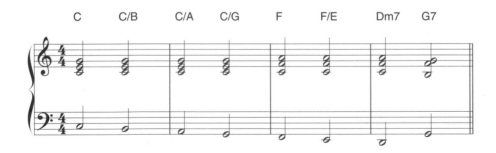

Figure 5-12. Bass movement as it would normally be indicated by slash chord symbols. Note that the "C/B" chord is actually a Cmaj7, a fact not reflected in the chord symbol. Likewise, the chord shown as "C/A" is actually an Am7, but many arrangers will use "C/A" instead in this situation because it makes the movement of the bass line more apparent when musicians are reading from a chord chart rather than reading notation.

# PROGRESSIONS USING 7TH CHORDS

Even in music that uses mostly triads, it's very common to play the dominant chord as a dominant 7th in a cadence leading to the tonic (see Figure 5-13). The plain dominant triad actually sounds a bit colorless and vague compared to the dominant 7th. To hear this for yourself, turn back to Figure 4-10 on page 62 and replace all the G triads with G7 chords by adding an F to each G chord.

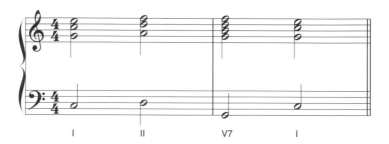

Figure 5-13. The V7 chord (a dominant 7th) is a staple of harmonic practice. Shown here is its most basic usage, preceding the tonic.

The movement from the dominant 7th to the tonic is such an important part of our harmonic vocabulary that composers quite often insert a dominant 7th before other major or minor chords. That is, they use not the main dominant 7th of the key (G7 in the key of C) but the dominant 7th chord that would be the dominant *in the key of the next chord.* In other words, if the upcoming chord in a piece in C major happens to be a D minor, the D minor chord can easily and appropriately be preceded by an A7 chord. The A7 is called a *secondary dominant,* because it's not the primary dominant of the key. Secondary dominants are among the more powerful resources in tonal music. A few simple examples of the use of secondary dominants are shown in Figure 5-14.

Figure 5-14. A secondary dominant can be used before any chord in a progression. Here, the basic progression (the chords appearing on beats 1 and 3 of each measure: C-Am-Dm-G) is enhanced through the use of three secondary dominants. The Am chord is preceded by an E7, which would be the dominant if the key of the piece were A minor. The Dm is preceded by an A7 in exactly the same way, and the G by a D7.

Note that a secondary dominant is never a strictly diatonic chord. It always contains one or more notes (accidentals) that are not part of the major scale implied by the key signature.

Rather than resolve a secondary dominant into its expected tonic chord, as in Figure 5-14, we can use a secondary dominant to precede another secondary dominant. This type of progression, shown in Figure 5-15, was especially common in Dixieland jazz. It gives the music a lot of forward momentum, because the unsettled energy of the dominant chord type doesn't resolve for several bars. However, the association with Dixieland is so strong that today this progression tends to sound somewhat old-fashioned.

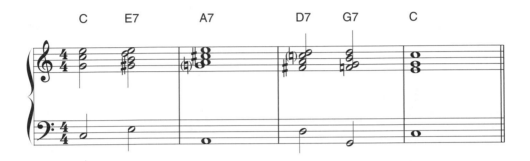

Figure 5-15. A string of secondary dominants, each leading to the next. E7 is the dominant of A, A7 the dominant of D, and so on. The resolution of the progression is delayed until the tonic is finally reached in measure 4.

Jazz musicians working in more modern styles carry the idea of secondary dominants one step further. In jazz, any chord in a progression can potentially be preceded by both the IIm7 and the V7 that would be used if the upcoming chord were the tonic. This is called "back-cycling," because it utilizes movement around the Circle of Fifths (see below). Figure 5-16 gives a simple example of back-cycling.

In Figure 5-17, the ideas in Figures 5-15 and 5-16 are combined. Each IIm7-V7 progression leads directly to the next one, as the I following each V7 becomes a IIm7 in the next part of the progression. Variations on this concept are used in many of the standard tunes played by jazz musicians – "Autumn Leaves" is a classic example. If you can dig up a chart for "Autumn Leaves," analyze it to find the IIm7-V7 progressions. Jazz players, by the way, normally refer to this type of progression as a "two-five." The fact that the first chord is some variety of minor 7th and the second some type of dominant 7th is understood.

So far we've been focusing exclusively on minor 7th and dominant 7th chords. Figures 5-16 and 5-17 use ordinary major triads for the C and F chords. In many or most jazz tunes, however, unadorned triads are rarely heard. (Odd as it

*Figure 5-16. A progression in C major in which each of the main chords (C, Am, F, and Dm) is preceded by its own IIm7-V7 progression. In essence, each of the main chords has become a temporary tonic chord in a different key. While the listener can hear the overall C major key of the progression, the added accidentals give this passage a stronger appeal than if it were written strictly with notes drawn from the C major scale.*

may seem, a straight triad may be heard as dissonant in a harmonic context that consists of 7th chords and other extended chord types.) Figure 5-17 would more likely be played as shown in Figure 5-18, with major 7th chords substituting for the major triads.

Based on what was said earlier about the strong tendency of a dominant 7th chord to move to its tonic, you might be surprised to learn that in jazz and blues, a dominant 7th is felt to be a consonant chord, not one that is dissonant or requiring resolution. In blues and blues-derived rock songs, *all* of the chords may be dominant 7ths. This has been true since the mid-1930s, when the hard-pounding piano style known as boogie-woogie popularized bass figures like the one in Figure 5-19. A few of the more common varieties of blues changes are discussed in Chapter Eight.

*Figure 5-17. Continuing the ideas in Figures 5-15 and 5-16, we can create a progression in which each IIm7-V7 is followed immediately by another, delaying the resolution until measure 3. Looking at the progression backwards, we could say that each of the IIm7 chords (after the first one) is preceded by its own IIm7-V7.*

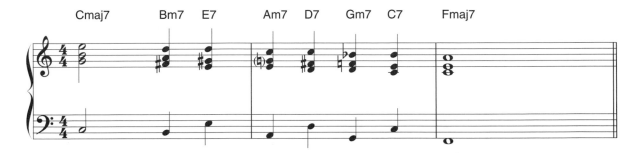

Figure 5-18. This progression is identical to the one in Figure 5-17, except that major 7th chords are used in place of the major triads in bars 1 and 3. The consistent use of 7th chords is more characteristic of the types of jazz where this sort of progression would be used.

We've already seen a few examples in which one chord was *substituted* for another (for example, the deceptive cadence shown in Chapter Four). Jazz musicians, however, have discovered and explored many ways of substituting one chord for another. Some will be discussed later in this book, and you may be able to learn others by listening or playing your instrument. One substitution that uses the dominant 7th is both simple enough and important enough to be worth explaining here.

Figure 5-19. This left-hand pattern is one of the staples of boogie-woogie piano, a blues-oriented style that was popular in the 1930s and 1940s. Boogie-woogie was one of the precursors of rock and roll. A dominant 7th chord is outlined by the root and 7th played on the third beat of each bar.

This substitution goes by several names. It can be called a flat-five substitution, an aug-four substitution, or a tritone substitution. Whatever you choose to call it, the idea is the same: In certain circumstances, a dominant 7th chord can be replaced with a different dominant 7th whose root is a tritone (an augmented 4th or diminished 5th) away from the root of the original chord.

Take a look at the two progressions in Figure 5-20. The first and third chords are identical, but in place of the expected dominant 7th chord in (a), I've substituted a D♭7 chord. D♭ is an augmented 4th away from the original root, G. The

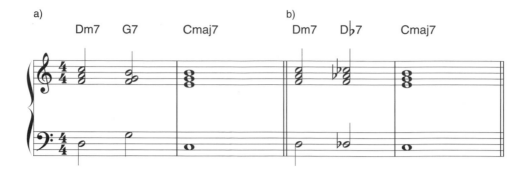

Figure 5-20. In jazz, it's usually possible to replace a dominant 7th chord with another dominant 7th whose root is a tritone away from the original root. Here, a standard II-V-I progression is shown in (a). The progression in (b) is identical except that a D♭7 chord has been substituted for the G7.

Figure 5-21. Another tritone substitution. This progression is identical to the one in Figure 5-15, except that an A♭7 has been substituted for the D7.

same idea is used in Figure 5-21. This example is almost identical to Figure 5-15, where each dominant 7th (from E7 through D7) is a secondary dominant in relation to the following root. However, in Figure 5-21 the D7 chord has been replaced by an A♭7. The root of the A♭7 is an augmented 4th away from the root of D7.

## THE CIRCLE OF FIFTHS

As Figure 5-15 shows, it's possible to string together a series of dominant 7th chords in which each chord is the dominant in relation to the root of the next chord. If we string together 12 chords in this manner, the chord roots will move through all 12 notes of the chromatic scale, and we'll find ourselves back where we started. Such a progression, which is shown in Figure 5-22, is not very satisfying, because it provides no clue about which note is the tonic. We seem to be entirely at sea.

*Figure 5-22. Each dominant 7th chord in this progression is preceded by its own secondary dominant. The progression moves through all 12 roots in the chromatic scale without ever arriving at a resting place. (Note that F♯7 is the enharmonic equivalent of G♭7. Technically, D♭7 is the dominant of G♭, not of F♯.)*

The roots of the chords in Figure 5-22 are all separated from one another by an interval of a 5th. If we plot them on a circle (to show the endless nature of the progression), we'll have the classic diagram in Figure 5-23. This diagram is called the Circle of Fifths. Some people prefer the term "Cycle of Fifths."

The Circle of Fifths is well worth studying and understanding. For one thing, it shows the arrangement of key signatures given in Chapter One. Each time we add a sharp to the key signature, or remove a flat, we move clockwise around the

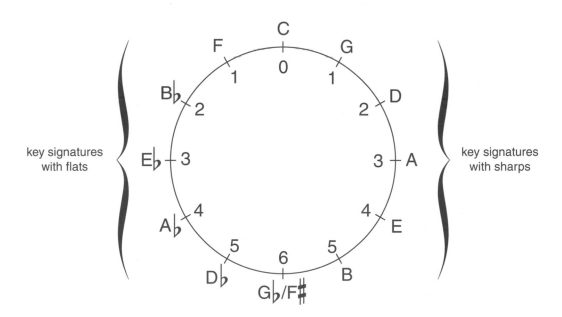

*Figure 5-23. The Circle of Fifths. The numbers inside the circle refer to the number of flats (on the left) or sharps (on the right) in the major key signature.*

Circle of Fifths. For example, from C to G we add one sharp (F♯), and from E♭ to B♭ we remove one flat (A♭). Conversely, when moving counterclockwise around the Circle of Fifths, we remove one sharp from the key signature, or add one flat to it. For example, when the key changes from A to D we remove one sharp (G♯).

The sharps and flats that are added to key signatures also follow the Circle. The new sharp added to a key signature on the right half of the Circle is always the note two steps counterclockwise from the key. The new sharp added to the key of A, for instance, is G♯. The new flat added to a key signature with flats, on the other hand, is always the note one step counterclockwise. When moving from the key of F, for instance (whose only flat is B♭) to the key of B♭, we add an E♭ to the key signature.

The notes directly opposite one another on the Circle are separated by the interval of a tritone. And both the notes in a diminished 7th chord and the notes in an augmented triad are easy to spot on the Circle, because the notes form regular geometrical shapes (a square and an equilateral triangle, respectively).

The roots of each IIm7-V7-I progression lie next to one another on the circle. For instance, if the first chord is a Bm7, we can find the next two by moving counterclockwise from B to E and then to A. The full progression would be Bm7-E7-A. This type of chord movement, counterclockwise around the Circle, is what jazz musicians refer to as "back-cycling."

## 7TH CHORD VOICINGS

Like the triads discussed in Chapter Three, 7th chords can be voiced in various ways. In fact, as the number of notes in the chord increases, the number of voicings available increases exponentially. A number of voicings of 7th chords have been used in the examples in this chapter, but most of them have been closed voicings. To learn to use 7th chords, you should spend a little time at the keyboard trying out alternate voicings, such as those shown in Figure 5-24.

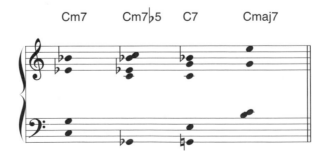

*Figure 5-24. A few ways, chosen more or less at random, in which 7th chords can be voiced.*

You may have noticed that in some of the examples used earlier in this chapter, the 5th was omitted from 7th chord voicings. This is a very common practice. The 5th contributes less to the characteristic sound of a straight 7th chord (whether it's a dominant 7th, a minor 7th, or a major 7th). The root can't usually be omitted, because if it is the voicing becomes ambiguous, as shown in Figure 5-25. If the 7th is omitted, the chord becomes an ordinary triad. And if the 3rd is omitted, the listener has no way to determine whether the chord is major or minor — an important factor in figuring out the meaning of a particular chord or progression. So when it becomes desirable to lighten up a chord voicing by leaving something out, the 5th is the first note to go.

Figure 5-25. When the root is eliminated from a 7th chord, what remains is a triad with a different root. It's useful to take a look at the type of triad created by the upper three voices. In a V7 chord, for instance, the upper voices are the diminished triad built on the leading tone of the major scale. In an earlier chapter, we noted that this triad is seldom used by itself. When placed above a V root, however, it becomes extremely useful. The upper voices of other 7th chords form augmented, major, and minor triads, as shown. The upper voices of the 7♭5 and 7♯5 chords (see Figure 5-28) don't form functional triads.

Assuming the bass player is playing the root, the keyboard player is free to drop both the root and 5th. This results in a partial chord voicing that contains only the 3rd and the 7th. This versatile voicing, shown in Figure 5-26, has been widely used in jazz comping (accompaniment) since the 1940s, if not before. It's most often seen when the sheet music calls for some type of dominant 7th chord. What's interesting and useful about this particular partial voicing is that when the composer or arranger calls for a tritone substitution of a dominant-type chord, for

Figure 5-26. This voicing of a G7 chord contains neither the root nor the 5th. The sound of the tritone is strong enough, however, to indicate the identity of the chord.

example a D♭7 chord in place of a G7, the two notes in the 3rd/7th partial voicing will be exactly the same: F and B. (In a D♭7 chord, the latter note is spelled enharmonically as a C♭ rather than a B, but this makes no difference in performance.) As Figure 5-27 shows, the bass player can move freely to either root: The voicing works either way. In the case of more complex dominant voicings, this trick may not always work, but it's well worth committing to memory.

*Figure 5-27. When a dominant 7th chord is voiced with neither a root nor a 5th, it can be used with either root in a tritone substitution.*

## ALTERING SINGLE NOTES

In showing you new chords that can be formed by stacking 3rds, I've been using only major and minor 3rds. Up to this point I've been scrupulously avoiding augmented and diminished 3rds in order to keep the discussion clear and simple. In fact, it's possible to stack either augmented 3rds or diminished 3rds, but if you do so, the resulting intervals would be better described either as perfect 4ths or as major 2nds, respectively. These chords, while useful, will be discussed in Chapter Six. A more useful way to think about chords based on stacked 3rds is to consider each note of the chord independently. The 3rd of the chord, for instance, can be either major (an E♮ in a C chord) or minor (an E♭ in a C chord). The 7th will usually be either major or minor, but in the diminished 7th chord it can be diminished. The 5th has three possible forms: It can be perfect, augmented, or diminished.

If you look at it this way, you'll discover that a few possibilities were left out of Figures 5-2 and 5-4. A more complete menu of 7th chord types would also have to include the chords in Figure 5-28. Both of these chords include a diminished 3rd interval — from E to G♭ in the first chord and from G♯ to B♭ in the second.

What about the 7th chords in Figure 5-29? While these chords are allowed by the rules set forth in this chapter, they're not used as often. When used, they're usually called something else. Try playing them and you'll hear why. The nominal root of these chords doesn't truly sound like a root. The chords have a bitonal or

Figure 5-28. Two more 7th chords. These are both dominant-type chords, but in both the 5th has been altered. As a result, one of the stacked 3rds in the chord is diminished.

ambiguous quality. As we go on, in the next chapter, to explore more complex chords, we'll encounter (or pass by quietly without mentioning them) many more chords that are in this category.

It's a bit difficult to put your finger on what makes one type of C 7th chord sound like a C chord while another sounds like something else. And in fact, musicians 50 years from now might answer the question differently than we would today. Harmonic practice evolves over time. Sounds that were fresh and exciting in one generation get "used up." To a later generation they begin to seem old and tired — clichés, in other words. Because of this fact, the ideas presented in this book are not the last word on the subject. Rather, they're a framework within and around which you can find harmonic resources that work for your own music.

Figure 5-29. These 7th chords are theoretically possible, but they wouldn't usually be analyzed as shown here. The first two chords would more likely be heard as a rootless D13 and D13♭9, respectively. The third chord is probably a bitonal voicing containing both A♭ major and A♭ minor triads, but it could also be analyzed as a D13♭9♭5 with no root or 3rd. The last chord is unambiguously an A♭add9 in first inversion. All of these chord types are discussed in Chapter Six.

# QUIZ

1. Name the seven basic types of 7th chords, and write them out using E as the root.

2. What is another name for the half-diminished 7th chord?

3. How many diminished 7th chords are there in all in the chromatic scale, assuming that enharmonically equivalent spellings are considered identical?

4. What chord traditionally follows a dominant chord?

5. What are the notes in a Cm7? In an Amaj7? In an F7?

6. If there is no number in a chord symbol, what type of chord is it?

7. Which note can be most easily omitted from 7th chord voicings?

8. Which chord would you substitute for a B♭7 chord in a tritone substitution?

9. What note should be voiced as the lowest note if the chart says to play a D7/C? An E/D♯?

10. Which secondary dominants in the key of C are diatonic with respect to the C major scale?

11. What triad is found in the upper three voices of a D7 chord? An E♭m-maj7? An F♯m7?

12. If you see the chord symbol "Gm/F," what note would you play in the bass? Considering all of the notes, what type of chord would you be playing?

# 6

# EXTENDED CHORDS

Since stacking another 3rd on top of a triad to create a 7th chord is so musically useful, why stop there? Why not stack a few more 3rds and see what happens?

This is exactly what classical composers started doing in the late 19th century. In the initial stages of the exploration of these chords, the higher notes (see Figure 6-1) were usually appoggiaturas, and resolved upward or downward to one of the tones in a triad or 7th chord. Even as early as Beethoven, however, the appoggiaturas sometimes went unresolved. According to Piston, whose outlook is conservative, "It is . . . essential in the nondominant ninth chord, as well as in the chords of the eleventh and thirteenth, that the character of these higher factors, as contrapuntal tones whose resolution is only implied, be recognized." In other words, academic authorities tend to feel that in the music of the 19th century, 9th, 11th, and 13th chords were not considered "real" chords in their own right: They were assumed to be dissonances that would resolve, even when the resolution never actually occurred in a given piece. Today, however, the idea that a chord containing a 9th, 11th, or 13th implies a resolution is entirely obsolete. These chords stand on their own.

During the 20th century, jazz composers and arrangers took the idea of stacking 3rds to heights no classical composer had ever dreamed of. The harmonic language they developed is both powerful and flexible. Stacking 3rds is only one part of this language, but it's the foundation on which other parts are built.

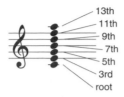

*Figure 6-1. By continuing to stack 3rds, as discussed in Chapters Three and Five, we can generate a harmonic framework that includes notes a 9th, an 11th, and a 13th above the root. This chord voicing is seldom used in the form shown here; rather, this is a framework from which a variety of real-world voicings can be derived.*

The structure shown in Figure 6-1, which contains three new stacked 3rds above the 7th chord framework, is the prototypical 13th chord. It contains seven of the 12 notes in the chromatic scale, which gives it a rather thick sound. The 13th chord is seldom used in this form, however. Instead, it's altered in various ways. The choice of which alterations to use depends on the harmonic context (what other chords are being played before and after) and the taste of the composer.

Two things are worth noting about Figure 6-1. First, there's no need to go past the 13th. If we stack another 3rd on top of the 13th, we'll be back at the root. (In some extended, quasi-bitonal voicings, this is not strictly true, but at the moment we're establishing a clear theoretical framework, not diving into the deep end of the pool.) Second, unlike the lower four notes of the stacked chord, the 9th, 11th, and 13th are more than an octave above the root. Based on the discussion of open and closed voicings in earlier chapters, you might expect that the 13th chord could be "folded inward" as shown in Figure 6-2 to create a closed voicing. It's very possible to construct chords along these lines, but whether such a chord would be considered a 13th chord or a cluster-chord (see "Other Chord Tones," near the end of this chapter) depends on the harmonic context.

For now, we're going to assume that the 9th, 11th, and 13th of a chord will normally be more than an octave above the chord root, and that the arrangement shown in Figure 6-1 is a closed voicing. The reason why higher elements in the stack of 3rds are almost always positioned in the the upper voices of a chord is discussed below, in the section "Voicings Using 9ths, 11ths, and 13ths."

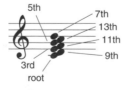

*Figure 6-2. In theory, the stacked 3rds in Figure 6-1 could be collapsed into a single octave, like this. However, such a structure makes it difficult to hear and identify the various notes of the chord, so the voicing in Figure 6-1 should be considered closed, not open.*

## 9TH CHORDS

The first new note added in Figure 6-1 is the 9th, which is a 3rd above the 7th. Because the 9th is the same scale step as the 2nd, it's a modal step, which means it comes in two basic flavors: major and minor. Accordingly, the menu of 9th chords includes both major 9th and minor 9th types. Chords with an augmented 9th are also used. Since there are seven different 7th chords, and any of three different 9ths can be stacked on any of them, you might think I'm about to list 21 different 9th chords. Some of the chords that would be in such a list are in common use, but others are almost never heard. The most often-used 9th chords are shown in Figure 6-3.

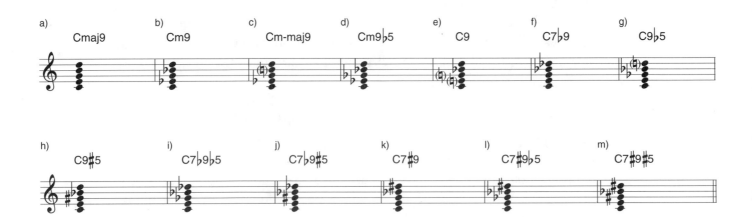

Figure 6-3. The most commonly used 9th chords. The first chord is a major type, chords (b) and (c) are minor, (d) is half-diminished, and (e) through (m), all of which have a major 3rd and a minor 7th, are dominants.

The main reason why other 9th chords, though theoretically possible, are not used is because they wouldn't sound like 9th chords. Like the never-used 7th chords shown at the end of the previous chapter, they would sound harmonically ambiguous — some other note in the chord would sound more like the root — or just plain dissonant. Consider, for instance, the painful chords in Figure 6-4. I'll leave you to work out some of the other seldom-used 9th chords for yourself.

The chords in Figure 6-3 fall naturally into four categories: major, minor, half-diminished, and dominant. The Cmaj9 chord is the only major-type chord in the group. Two of the chords, Cm9 and Cm-maj9, are minor. Cm9♭5 is half-diminished, because of the lowered 3rd and 5th. The other nine chords are all dominants. This trend will continue as we look at other chords: There tend to be more dominants than other types. This may have to do with the fact that the framework

Figure 6-4. These chords are seldom used. While technically they're both 9th chords with a C root, they sound dissonant or bitonal. The first chord is dissonant because of the half-step collisions between the root (C) and both the major 7th and minor 9th. The second chord is confusing because the upper voices form an E♭7 chord. This chord is so strong that it overpowers our sense of the C as a root.

of the dominant 7th chord (the root, 3rd, and 7th) gives the chord a stronger aural focus, so that more types of notes can be added without obscuring its underlying identity.

The nine dominant chords in Figure 6-3 are formed by varying only two of the notes – the 5th and the 9th – while the framework of the root, 3rd, and 7th remains fixed. The 5th can be natural, diminished, or augmented; the 9th can be minor, major, or augmented.

As with 7th chords, if a note is dropped from a 9th chord to create a more open voicing, it will usually be the 5th. If the chord chart calls for a ♯5 or ♭5, however, dropping the 5th would obscure the composer's or arranger's intentions, so the 5th is usually played in these chords.

As an addendum to Figure 6-3, we need to at least glance at chords in which the 5th or 9th is *split*. Because the ♭9 and ♯9 are a whole-step apart, including them both in a chord can sound good. The same goes for the ♭5 and ♯5. These chords are shown in Figure 6-5. In fact, the split 5th can be used in a dominant 7th chord rather than a 9th chord, producing a 7♯5♭5.

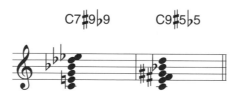

Figure 6-5. A couple of examples of chords in which the 5th or 9th is split. The C7♯9♭9 contains both minor and augmented 9ths, and the C7♯5♭5 contains both augmented and diminished 5ths. Rather than use the same letter-name for both 5ths or both 9ths, some arrangers will spell one of the notes enharmonically. In particular, the augmented 9th is often spelled as if it were a minor 3rd. Perhaps this is because the notation, which requires an accidental on the major 3rd, provides a more accurate reflection of the aural clash between the 3rd and the augmented 9th.

# MORE ABOUT CHORD SYMBOLS

As we add more notes to our chord voicings, the chord symbols used will naturally get longer and harder to read. They're still constructed using some basic rules, however. To expand on the list of rules laid out in the last chapter:

**1.** If the chord symbol uses "maj," it contains both a major 3rd and a major 7th.

**2.** If it uses "m," it contains both a minor 3rd and a minor 7th.

**3.** If it contains neither "maj" nor "m," but does contain a number, it's a dominant-type chord: It has a major 3rd and a minor 7th.

**4.** The highest note in the closed voicing (in Figure 6-3, this is the 9th) is always mentioned.

**5.** It's assumed that all of the notes below the highest are also present, whether or not they're mentioned – though in an actual playing situation one or more of them might be dropped to create a more open voicing. Thus, any chord that is identified as being a 9th chord has a 7th, even if the 7th is not mentioned in the chord symbol. This is the case with the Cmaj9, Cm9, and C9 chords in Figure 6-3, for instance. Because of rule 3, above, we can tell that the 7th in a C9 is a minor 7th. In other words, a C9 is a dominant 7th chord type.

In the case of the 13th chord, however, this rule is relaxed slightly: When the symbol includes a 13, the chord is assumed to contain both a 7th and a 9th, but not an 11th. The 11th is such an oddball note that it should be mentioned explicitly if it's to be played. (An alternate way to interpret "11" and "13" in chord symbols is given below in the section "Other Chord Tones.")

**6.** A note that is not mentioned is assumed to have its normal, unaltered pitch. If the 5th is not mentioned, for instance, a perfect 5th (neither augmented nor diminished) should be played. This is the case with the first, second, fifth, and sixth chords in Figure 6-3. Because of rule 3, the "normal, unaltered" pitch of the 7th is a minor 7th, not a major 7th.

**7.** Flat and sharp symbols are used to indicate notes that are a half-step above or below their unaltered pitch. This is the case even when the accidental of the note being played is not, in fact, a flat or sharp. The ♭9 in an F♯♭9 chord, for instance, is a G♮, not a G♭.

**8.** Flat and sharp symbols are never used to indicate the position of the 3rd and 7th, because those notes are specified by "maj" and "m."

**9.** It's not possible to use a ♭ or ♯ to indicate an altered note immediately after the chord root, because this would create an ambiguous chord symbol. The symbol C♭9, for instance, could indicate either a C chord with a ♭9 or a dominant 9th chord whose root is C♭. (The latter interpretation is correct.) Because of this potential ambiguity, it's sometimes necessary to mention notes in the chord symbol that would not otherwise need to be mentioned. This is generally the case with chords that include a ♭9 or some higher altered note, such as a ♯11. These chords have to be abbreviated 7♭9 and so on, putting the "7" between the chord root letter and the accidental.

Conversely, if a chord symbol contains an accidental immediately after the chord name (for instance, E♭9), the accidental refers unambiguously to the root, *not* to the upper note indicated by the number.

As a matter of consistency, this rule is extended to cover even cases where the use of an accidental would not be ambiguous. For instance, the symbol "F♯♭9" unambiguously indicates a chord whose root is F♯, and which contains a flatted 9th. Even so, the symbol F♯7♭9 is easier to read.

Taken together, these rules explain all the details of the chord symbols in Figure 6-3. For instance, the C9 is a dominant-type chord (because it's neither "maj" nor "m"). The C9♭5 is a dominant-type chord, and has a 7th even though the 7th is not mentioned. Most confusingly, perhaps, the Cm9 chord is called a "minor 9" chord even though the 9th itself is major, not minor. (The 9th, remember, is a modal scale step, and comes in major and minor versions.) The "m" in this case refers to the 3rd and 7th, not the 9th.

As a practical matter, jazz musicians often interpret a chord symbol shown in sheet music as a straight dominant 7th chord (for example, F7 or B♭7) by adding a 9th, a 13th, or both. If the arranger wants a specific altered note, such as a ♭9 or a ♭5, it will be indicated in the chord symbol, but "7" is sometimes used as shorthand for "play a dominant-type voicing of your choice here." Don't try this in a country music session, though. In more traditional styles, the symbol "F7" means the notes F, A, C, and E♭, with no fooling around.

## 11TH CHORDS

Chords in which an 11th is stacked above the 9th are used from time to time, but they're less common than either 9th chords or 13th chords. There are two reasons for this. First, the natural 11th (which would be an F above a C root) interferes with our ability to hear the root of the chord, because it's the same note as the subdominant, which is a lower root. Also, it clashes with the major 3rd.

The voicings in Figure 6-6 show how out of place the natural 11th sounds against the major 3rd. These chords might be usable in some circumstances, but I'd tend to analyze them as bitonal (a G7 or B♭ chord above a C triad) rather than as 11th chords. The natural 11th can be combined with a 3rd in only one chord I can think of offhand — the m11 chord, which is shown in Figure 6-7.

The sharp 11th (see Figure 6-8) is more useful. However, this note is the same as the flat 5th. So when the performer in search of a more open voicing drops the natural 5th, a ♯11 chord becomes indistinguishable from a 9♭5 chord in which the

Figure 6-6. These 11th chords (Cmaj11 and C11) are not very useful, because of the natural 11th. Raising the 11th, as in Figure 6-8, produces a more viable sound.

Cm11

Figure 6-7. The natural 11th sounds good when combined with the minor 3rd and minor 7th.

Cmaj9♯11      C9♯11

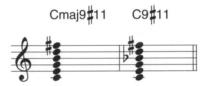

Figure 6-8. The sharp 11th sounds good with both major-type and dominant-type chords.

Figure 6-9. If the 5th is omitted from the chord voicing, the ♯11 is functionally indistinguishable from a ♭5. Because of this, some arrangers will use a ♯11 in the chord symbol only when they also want the unaltered 5th to be included in the voicing.

♭5 has been transposed up by an octave. Figure 6-9 illustrates this fact. So if the arranger calls for a ♯11 chord, it may be reasonable to assume the voicing is intended to include *both* a natural 5th and a ♯11. Alternatively, the arranger may assume the 5th will be dropped, and may be calling the note a ♯11 rather than a ♭5 to indicate that the 11th should be voiced at the top of the chord.

Based on the rules for chord symbols given above, you can quickly deduce two things about chord symbols for 11th chords. First, any chord called an 11 also includes a 9th and a 7th. Second, when the 11 is sharped, it can't be mentioned immediately after the root. (Would a "C♯11" be a C dominant chord with a ♯11, or would it be a C♯ chord with a natural 11th?) Thus, strange as it may seem, a chord symbol for a chord containing a ♯11 will always mention the 9th. If the 9th is flatted, as in C7♭9♯11, both the 7th and 9th need to be mentioned.

Some arrangers and music copyists, however, assume you're smart enough to know that except in a minor-type chord such as the m11, the 11th is usually sharped. If you see a chord symbol like "C11" or "G11" in a score, it may be safe to assume that a ♯11 chord is meant. Or it may not (see the discussion of sus chords in "Other Chord Tones," below).

## 13TH CHORDS

The 13th falls on a modal scale step, so it can be either major or minor. There's no such thing as a diminished or augmented 13th, however. The diminished 13th would be the same note as the perfect 5th, and the augmented 13th would be the same note as the flat 7th. Some useful 13th chords are shown in Figure 6-10. Note that some interior notes are dropped from the voicings in this figure. These voicings may or may not be the most commonly used 13th chords, but they sound better to my ears than most of the alternatives.

Note the exception to rule 5 in the rules for chord symbols mentioned earlier in this chapter. The presence of a 13 in the symbol does *not* imply that the chord also contains an 11th (though it does imply the 7th and most likely the 9th). If the arranger wants an 11th to be part of the 13th chord, it will be mentioned in the chord chart. However, performers who regularly work from chord charts that include chords of this sort give themselves considerable latitude to interpret the symbols in ways that feel right at the moment. If you're playing with jazz players and see a 13 chord in a chart, you may or may not want to play a 9th along with the 13th. In fact, depending on what the soloist is doing at the moment, you might easily play an altered 9th or altered 5th, even though the chart doesn't call for it.

*Figure 6-10. The 13th can be either major (as in the first, second, and fifth chords shown here) or minor (as in the third and fourth chords). The 13th is heard most often in dominant-type voicings (chords two through five) but also works nicely over a maj9♯11.*

## VOICINGS USING 9THS, 11THS & 13THS

With 7th chords, we were able to create inversions rather freely, by placing any of the notes in the chord in the bass. In general, it's not practical to do this with the 9th, 11th, and 13th. When placed in the lowest voice, these notes tend to obscure the harmonic identity of the chord. Consider, for instance, the rather unfortunate inversions shown in Figure 6-11. If the higher notes of the stack are below the root, the chord tends not to be perceived as a 9th, 11th, or 13th chord but as something else, probably a bitonal voicing (see below). In other words, there's no such thing as a fourth, fifth, or sixth inversion of a 13th chord. However, we can continue to put the 3rd, 5th, or 7th in the bass, as before. Figure 6-12 shows a few voicings (mostly inversions) that sound pleasant and are easily identifiable. These chords have been revoiced in other ways as well: Sometimes one or two notes have been dropped, and one or more notes may have been shifted up or down by an octave.

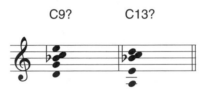

*Figure 6-11. While the root, 3rd, 5th, or 7th of a chord can easily be used in the bass, it's not practical to put the 9th, 11th, or 13th in the bass, as doing so interferes with our ability to identify the root. The chord on the left has all of the notes of a C9, but because the 9th is in the bass, it doesn't sound much like a functional C chord. The chord on the right is even more awkward: The open 5th interval at the bottom leads the ear to expect some type of A chord, but this is contradicted by the B♭ and D. This is not to say that voicings of this type are musically useless, however; see Figure 6-28.*

If you're new to the idea of using extended voicings like these, the choice of notes may seem almost arbitrary: Couldn't we choose just about any combination of notes and call it a C chord? Yes and no. Your ear may suggest voicings to you that other players have ignored or rejected — and if it works for you, nobody can really tell you you're wrong. On the other hand, there are some guidelines you may find helpful to bear in mind.

First, chords that use both the major 3rd and natural 4th/11th of the scale are somewhat adventurous, though they can work well, as Figure 6-13 illustrates.

Second, you'll rarely hear a major 9th used in the same chord with a minor or augmented 9th. The sound is just too dissonant.

Third, the higher functions of an extended chord are usually placed higher in the voicing. Play the first two voicings in Figure 6-14 and you'll hear why. The second voicing sounds a bit muddy, or at least darker, because the 13th is voiced

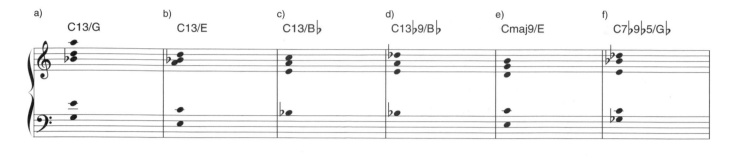

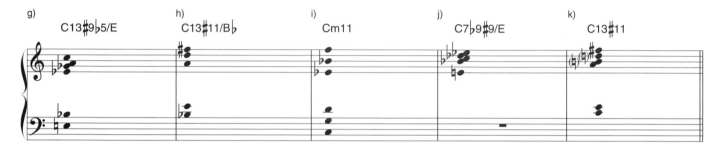

*Figure 6-12. An assortment of 9th, 11th, and 13th chord voicings. Using these voicings as a starting point, it's a useful exercise to try adding, omitting, octave-transposing, or altering various chord tones to find other voicings that are pleasing to your ear.*

*Figure 6-13. When the first chord in Figure 6-6 is revoiced a bit, it becomes surprisingly pleasant. Perhaps this is because the clash between the major 3rd and the natural 11th is less disturbing to the ear when they're in the same octave.*

in the lower octave, while the 7th is more than an octave above it. In the third voicing in this figure, the 9th has also been moved down an octave, swapping places with the 3rd, and the voicing has become a bit unstable. At least one jazz pianist, Clare Fischer, has used the trick of dropping higher chord notes down to lower positions in this manner to give his chords a more mysterious flavor, but there are reasons why the practice is not the norm.

Placing the augmented 9th in a lower octave than the major 3rd is probably a bad idea, because the ear will interpret the 9th as a minor 3rd. The augmented 9th

*Figure 6-14. Normally, the higher functions of a chord are placed higher in the voicing, but this principle can sometimes be violated with good results. The first C13 chord is in a "normal" configuration, with the 13th and 9th at the top. In the second chord, the 3rd and 9th have switched places. In the third chord, the 13th and 7th have switched places. In the last chord, both swaps have taken place. The third and fourth voicings are darker and more mysterious, but not bad at all. Try playing these voicings on the keyboard a few times, alternating them until you can hear the sounds as interchangeable.*

can be played in the same octave as the major 3rd, however, producing a half-step major-minor dissonance.

Fourth, as more notes are added to the voicing, the potential for harmonic confusion grows. This can be a good thing or a bad thing, depending on the musical context. To begin with, let's note that most extended chords contain all of the notes of one or more triads other than the triad built on the root of the chord. Look, for example, at the chords in Figure 6-12c, 6-12e, and 6-12h. In each case, the notes in the treble clef form a triad — A minor, G major, and D major, respectively. These triads clash with the underlying C tonality, but in an interesting way.

If we swap the right-hand notes in Figure 6-12e into the left hand and vice-versa, we get the awkward chord in Figure 6-15. What is this chord, harmonically speaking? It's hard to say. It has the same notes as the Cmaj9 in Figure 6-12e, but the sound of the G triad now dominates the voicing. The ear simply doesn't interpret this voicing as a C chord. Yet it doesn't sound functionally like a G chord either,

??

*Figure 6-15. This chord was created by swapping the left- and right-hand notes in the chord in Figure 6-12e. Although the notes are the same, moving the G major triad to the bottom gives us a voicing that is no longer identifiable as a C major chord. Its harmonic identity is not at all clear.*

*Figure 6-16. This chord was created by swapping the left- and right-hand notes in the chord in Figure 6-12g. The original voicing was bitingly thick, but could still be perceived by the ear as a C dominant. When the 13th, sharp 9th, and flat 5th are dropped down to a lower octave, the result is harmonic sludge.*

because of the prominent E-C interval. At best, we could call it a bitonal G/C chord. This is not to say that the voicing is useless — but if you play it when the chord chart calls for a Cmaj9, your fellow musicians will give you a few funny looks.

Still not convinced? Try swapping hands with the voicing in Figure 6-12g, moving the diminished 7th component down to the left hand, as shown in Figure 6-16. It's a harmonic train wreck.

When choosing the notes for a chord voicing, then, you need to be sensitive to internal combinations of notes (usually triads, tritones, or dissonant minor 2nds and minor 9ths) that may convey harmonic ideas you don't want. As long as you're following this principle, however, harmonic clashes can be a good thing. Consider the right-hand voicing in Figure 6-17. It's clearly a C dominant chord, at least to my ears. The A major triad (enharmonically spelled with a Db) is masked by the Bb and Eb, and doesn't create much ambiguity. The ear focuses mainly on the clashing half-steps.

*Figure 6-17. Dissonance doesn't always create harmonic ambiguity. If you don't play the C root in the left hand, the upper notes are not readily identifiable as a C voicing, but they don't imply any other root either. Note that the split accidental notes (Eb and E♮) are intended to be played at the same time. They're offset purely because of the limitations of our notation system.*

## AMBIGUOUS VOICINGS

In spite of the potential for confusion discussed above, harmonic ambiguity is not, in itself, a bad thing. On the contrary. Take a look at the right-hand voicing in Figure 6-18. This is an important voicing, one you'll hear often — but what is it? If we play a G in the root, it's clearly a G13 chord (though there's no 9th). If we play a Db root, on the other hand, the voicing is just as clearly a Db7#9. Figure 6-19 makes this clear.

*Figure 6-18. Can you identify this voicing? Hint #1: It doesn't contain a root or a 5th. Hint #2: The tritone between B and F indicates that you're looking for a dominant-type chord.*

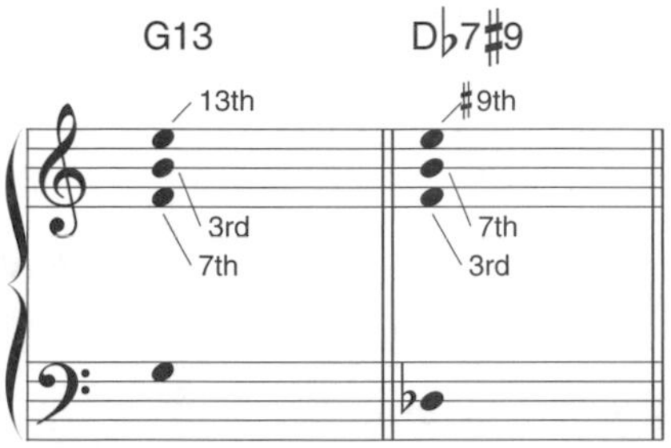

*Figure 6-19. The voicing in Figure 6-18 can function either as a G13 or as a Db7#9. (In the latter case, the 7th of the chord is spelled enharmonically as a B♮ rather than as a Cb, which would technically be the correct spelling.)*

In Chapter Five, we introduced the idea of the *tritone substitution*, in which a dominant-type chord is replaced with a different dominant-type chord whose root is a tritone away from the original root. To review, please glance back at Figures 5-26 and 5-27. In Figure 6-19, we've stacked a perfect 4th above the tritone, and then used tritone substitution to replace a G13 chord with a Db7#9. Yet if we play a rootless voicing, as a pianist or keyboard player would typically do, leaving the root for the bass player, the two chord voicings are identical.

This fact is worth exploring further. In Figure 6-20, a couple of variations on the voicing from Figure 6-18 are shown. In each case, a note has one identity in the G chord and a separate identity in the Db chord, yet none of the notes creates any undesirable harmonic ambiguities in either chord.

The world of jazz harmony is full of ambiguous chord voicings that work well. Another simple example is shown in Figure 6-21. Are these notes part of a C9 chord? A Bbmaj7? Or are they extracted from a Gm9? The answer is, "All of the above." They could be part of an F#7#9#5, for that matter. Take a look at how these notes are used in the riff in Figure 6-22. The A, Bb, and D don't change when the root moves from G to C. They work in both chords. (There's a bit more movement

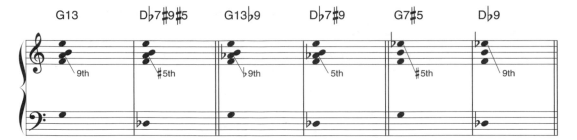

Figure 6-20. When playing a tritone substitution, it may not be necessary to change the upper notes of the chord voicing in any way. Shown here are three different ways of voicing either a G7-type chord or a D♭7-type chord.

Figure 6-21. Another ambiguous voicing. Lacking any other information, this would appear to be a B♭maj7 chord in third inversion — but see Figure 6-22.

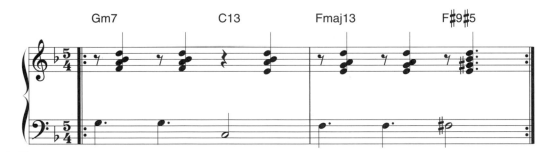

Figure 6-22. In this riff, the notes in Figure 6-21 are used to voice Gm7 and C13 chords. This riff illustrates a technique that is often used with extended voicings: Two or more notes may continue without changing through several different chords. As each new root is played, the notes acquire different harmonic identities.

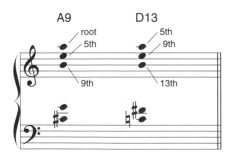

Figure 6-23. Another example in which three notes are sustained from one chord to another. If you have trouble hearing the second chord as a D, play the D root in a lower octave along with the voicing shown.

in measure 2. I've added this measure purely to show how such chords might appear in an arrangement.)

Note groups consisting of stacked 4ths are found in a number of 9th, 11th, and 13th chords. In Figure 6-23, for instance, the stacked 4th shape in the right hand remains fixed, while the two lower voices each drop by a half-step.

## OTHER CHORD TONES

Take a look at Figure 6-24. The chord on the second beat is clearly a C9 — but what are we to call the chord on the first beat? Possibly the F is an 11th. But remember what was said earlier about how the use of higher notes within a stack of 3rds implies the presence of lower notes. Remember also that the 3rd of a chord is one of the most important notes for establishing the identity of the chord. In some situations the 3rd is even more important than the root. So the chord on the first beat of this example is a puzzle: It has no 3rd.

Figure 6-24. A suspended 4th (the F) resolving downward to the 3rd of a C9 chord.

In this type of voicing, the F is called a *suspended 4th*. In chord symbols, this is abbreviated "sus4," and the popular term for chords that use suspended 4ths is "sus chords." Another way to look at this note would be as an augmented 3rd, but that terminology is never used, because there is no basic triad that contains an augmented 3rd. The note is considered "suspended" because it feels as if the voice playing the note is about to drop from the 4th down to the 3rd. This movement, in which the suspended 4th resolves downward, is shown in Figure 6-24.

The general rule is that a sus4 chord never contains a 3rd: It contains a 4th instead. It can contain any of the other tones in the 13th chord stack, but normally a sus4 will be a dominant-type chord. It would be rare to hear a suspended 4th in combination with a major 7th. To see why, look at Figure 6-25. The suspended 4th and major 7th form a tritone. As a result, we tend to hear the chord in this example not as a Cmaj9sus4 but as a G7/C. It's a useful chord, but it's not really a C chord.

*Figure 6-25. This might appear on paper to be a Cmaj9sus4 chord (the F 4th replacing the E 3rd), but perceptually, and therefore functionally, it's a G7 above a C root. The tritone interval between the F and B guides the ear to perceive the G dominant shape.*

A suspended 4th is usually in the middle of a chord voicing, or on top. When it's used in the bass, the identity of the chord root will be obscured. If the suspension resolves to the 3rd, however, it can be used in the bass, as in Figure 6-26.

*Figure 6-26. Normally a sus4 should not be used as the lowest note in a voicing, unless it resolves to the 3rd. On its own (assuming no bassist is playing the C), the C13sus4 chord here will be heard as a B♭maj7, not as a C chord. The movement from F down to E, however, makes it clear that we've been hearing a C13.*

If the sus4 is the top note in a C7sus4 voicing, some arrangers will call the chord a C11. I don't recommend this usage, because I feel the "11" in the symbol implies the presence of a 3rd. Another correct name for the chord would be B♭/C.

The term "suspended" seems to imply that the 4th will eventually resolve downward to the 3rd. In 19th-century classical music, such a resolution would have been all but inevitable, as the quote from *Harmony* at the beginning of this chapter suggests. But in more modern styles, no resolution of the suspended 4th is necessary. Progressions in which a sus4 chord leads directly to another chord are very practical. The next chord could even be another sus4 chord, as in Figure 6-27.

Figure 6-28 takes the idea of suspended 4ths and extends it a bit. I wrote this pattern in order to explore the possibility that the chords in Figure 6-11 might be more useful than they appear. I'm not entirely sure how to analyze the last chord in this figure, because it's right at the edge where functional harmony turns into bitonalism. But it's an interesting chord. Since there are an infinite number of ways to combine chords, this book couldn't possibly cover all of them, but

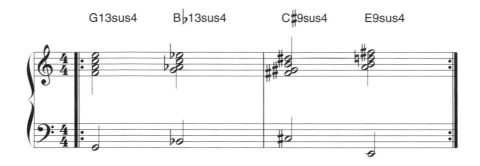

*Figure 6-27. This jazzy chord riff has no clear I chord — in other words, we can't quite say what key it's in — because the roots move through a series of minor 3rds. It illustrates an interesting way to use unresolved sus4 chords.*

*Figure 6-28. This Latin riff uses the unconventional inversions in Figure 6-11. Although the D9 is a dominant chord, in this riff it functions as the tonic, not as a dominant. The second chord can be analyzed as C7/D or as a D9sus4 with a B♭ slapped into the middle of it. Call it a D9♭13sus4 if you like. In the C7/A, this entire voicing is suspended over the A root. The A root implies a dominant in the key of D, but most of the expected dominant notes are missing. If you analyze this chord as an A7♯9♭9 with no 3rd, I won't argue with you, but calling it a C7/A is easier and arguably says more about the actual sound of the chord. Note that this same riff will sound much more normal (and perhaps less interesting) if you replace the B♭'s with A's.*

perhaps this figure will inspire you to dream up some outlandish progressions of your own.

Next, consider the much more conventional chord in Figure 6-29. There are two ways to analyze this chord, both of them correct: We can call it an Am7 in first inversion (the notes A-C-E-G with the C in the bass), or we can look at it as a C major triad with an extra note a 6th above the root – an *added 6th.* When the C is the lowest note, the major triad has such a strong sound that the latter interpretation makes more sense. The major 6th chord was used a lot in jazz and pop in the 1930s, but today it sounds old-fashioned, and tends to be avoided except when the arranger wants to throw in something sweet or corny.

*Figure 6-29. The major 6th chord (in this case, C6) contains the same notes as a minor 7th chord (Am7) in first inversion.*

If the chord contains no notes except a major triad and an added 6th, the chord symbol is simple: The chord in Figure *6-29* is called a C6. But the 6th is the same note of the scale as the 13th. So why not call this chord a C13? Because the existence of a 13th would imply the existence of a 7th (definitely), 9th (probably), and 11th (possibly). In the absence of these upper notes, it makes much more sense, both to make it easier to interpret the chord symbol and in terms of how we hear the chord, to consider the note a 6th.

When you want to add a tone to a chord, but you don't want to call it a 9th, 11th, or 13th because you don't want to imply the presence of other tones, the way to do it is with the handy term "add." The first chord in Figure 6-30, for instance, is a simple C major triad to which a 2nd (D) has been added: It's an add2 chord. If the chord had a 7th, we could call it a C9, because the D would be the 9th of such a chord. But since there's no 7th, the correct abbreviation is Cadd2. We could just as easily call it a Cadd9, because "add" means "this isn't a real 9th, it's just a note that has been grafted on." If the note one step above the root is added, it's a matter of taste whether to call the chord an add2 or an add9. I've seen pop songwriters use the symbol C2 for this chord. There's nothing wrong with this symbol except that it doesn't quite fit into any system.

The "add" nomenclature can be used to add a 4th to a chord. If the chord were called an 11 rather than an add4 (or add11), it would imply the presence of a 7th and 9th.

In the absence of any other information in the chord symbol, the 6th is always major. A chord containing only a triad and a minor 6th will normally be called an add♭6 or add♭13.

## FOURTH-CHORDS

Since stacking 3rds leads to so many harmonic possibilities, it's natural to wonder what might happen when we stack other intervals. Stacking 2nds (as in Figure 6-31) yields a variety of structures known as *cluster-chords.* Cluster-chords can be used to create dissonances, but there's no easy way to string them together in meaningful chord progressions.

Stacking 4ths is a bit more interesting. A stack of three or more 4ths is called a *fourth-chord.* Fourth-chords are somewhat ambiguous tonally: When a progres-

Figure 6-30. When an extra note needs to be added to a voicing, the notation "add" is used in the chord symbol. The 6 chord is technically an "add" chord, but if the major 6th is the only added note, there's no need to clutter up the chord symbol: Calling it a 6 chord does the trick. The third chord here can't be called a C7sus4, because a sus4 chord contains no 3rd (the E), and it can't be called a C11 because there's no 9th (D). The "add4" notation correctly indicates the clash between the 3rd and 4th.

Figure 6-31. A cluster-chord built out of stacked 2nds can be useful for injecting some dissonance into a texture. Depending on the surrounding harmonic context, the voicing shown might (or might not) be heard as a Cmaj9 chord — in other words, as a chord constructed using stacked 3rds, voiced in an unusually closed position.

sion is written using fourth-chords, it's not usually possible to say what key it's in. This effect can be seen in Figure 6-32. While the progression has a clear sense of harmonic movement, it lacks a tonal center. In fact, it's not even possible to say what the root of a fourth-chord is with any certainty, because it contains neither of the notes found in a triad (the 3rd and 5th) that help us identify the root of the triad. Accordingly, there are no accepted names or chord symbols for fourth-chords. Some theorists feel that the second note in a fourth-chord, counting up from the bottom, feels like the root.

It's also possible to stack 5ths or 7ths. From the fact that a 5th is an inverted 4th and a 7th is an inverted 2nd, you might expect that stacked 5ths would have

Figure 6-32. When a chord is formed by stacking 5ths, the bottom note will usually be perceived as the root, even though the chord has no 3rd.

*Figure 6-33. As with stacked 5ths, chords formed by stacking 7ths will be usually be interpreted as having the root on the bottom.*

the same harmonic effect as stacked 4ths, and stacked 7ths the same effect as stacked 2nds. But there's a difference, as Figures 6-32 and 6-33 show. In chords built using stacked 5ths or 7ths, the lowest note is easily perceptible as the root. A chord built by stacking 6ths can always be analyzed as a conventional chord containing stacked 3rds, but with an open voicing.

The 4ths in a fourth-chord are usually perfect 4ths. If any of them is augmented or diminished, the chord becomes easier to hear and analyze as an extended stacked-3rds chord with one or more altered or suspended notes. You can create useful voicings this way, but whether to call them fourth-chords becomes a matter

*Figure 6-34. A chromatic progression using fourth-chords. Fourth-chords lack a clearly perceptible root, so they aren't usually indicated with chord symbol abbreviations.*

*Figure 6-35. Altering a single note within a fourth-chord will usually turn it into some sort of stacked-3rds voicing. Here, the lower note (left) and second note (right) are altered.*

*Figure 6-36. More 4ths can be stacked, producing a more intense sound. In some big-band jazz charts, this type of voicing is used in a sustained chord at the very end of the piece, with a shrieking trumpet playing the very top note. More and more instruments can be added one by one to the top of the chord (E♭, A♭, and so on), producing a dense and towering sonority.*

of personal preference. Starting with the first chord in Figure 6-34, for instance, we can try raising and lowering each tone in turn to see what sort of harmony results. Doing this to the lower two notes gives us the voicings in Figure 6-35. As you can see, these chords are not hard to analyze as combinations of stacked 3rds.

Stacking more 4ths gives us a chord structure that's more intense, and also more harmonically ambiguous, as Figure 6-36 shows. The clash between the low A and the high B♭ in this chord is especially jarring.

Fourth-chords are most often played in close position, as in Figure 6-36, rather than being revoiced with various notes in other octaves. Sometimes one of the notes is moved up or down by an octave, but when we start moving individual notes up and down, any fourth-chord with six or fewer notes becomes analyzable as a conventional stacked-3rds chord. The fourth-chord in Figure 6-35, for instance, which is shown with no chord symbol, is actually analyzable as an F7sus4. This will become clear if you move the C up an octave. Likewise, the six-note stack in Figure 6-36 can be analyzed as a B♭maj9add6. To hear this a bit better, switch the octaves of the B♭ and the A. For that matter, the stacked 2nds in Figure 6-30 are readily analyzable as a Cmaj9.

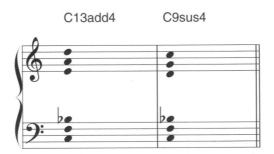

C13add4          C9sus4

*Figure 6-37. Slipping an augmented 4th (left) or a major 3rd (right) into the middle of a fourth-chord can produce some useful voicings.*

What this means is that if you want a fourth-chord to be perceived as a fourth-chord, or a cluster-chord to be perceived as a cluster-chord, your options for revoicing it are limited.

Fourth-chords are a limited resource, but they're well worth experimenting with. For instance, rather than alter a single note, as in Figure 6-35, we can insert an augmented 4th or a major 3rd into the middle of the stack, and then go on adding perfect 4ths above it. A couple of possibilities are shown in Figure 6-37.

## BITONAL CHORDS

What is the chord shown in Figure 6-38? One way of analyzing it is as a Cmaj13#11 with no 7th. If we look at it this way, the A is the 13th of the chord, the F# the #11, and the D the 9th. But this analysis seems needlessly academic. What we're really hearing are a C major triad and a D major triad played at the same time — two separate chords, each with its own root, 3rd, and 5th. Since each triad has its own tonal center (the root), harmonic structures built in this manner are called *bitonal*. Bitonality is not restricted to combining triads; bitonal writing containing 7ths, 9ths, and other notes is quite practical.

The use of bitonality became important in classical music in the early 20th century, and it remains an important harmonic resource for many classical composers. Whole passages are sometimes written in which one instrument or group of instruments plays in one key, while a different instrument or group plays in another key. To an unsophisticated listener, the results can be jarringly discordant, but as you gain familiarity with bitonal sonorities, you may find it possible to tease out the various harmonic strands and thereby make a lot more sense of the music.

*Figure 6-38. This bitonal chord consists of independent C major and D major triads.*

Consider, for example, the bitonal riff in Figure 6-39. At any given moment, the intervals between the left and right hands are likely to be quite dissonant — the C and C# played together on the first beat, for instance. But if you play this passage a couple of times, its inner logic should become easier to hear. Each hand is playing a simple V-I progression, but the right hand is playing in the key of B, while the left hand plays in the key of F.

Swing eighths

*Figure 6-39. In this bitonal passage, the two lines are in different keys. (Note the key signatures.) The right hand plays a V-I progression in the key of B, while the left hand also plays a V-I progression with the same harmonic rhythm, but in the key of F.*

This passage illustrates an important aspect of bitonalism: It's sometimes used in multi-part writing in which various instruments play passages that are not, considered in isolation, bitonal. The bitonalism is a result of the combination of parts. The parts may not be notated with separate key signatures, however. Accidentals are normally employed. Also, there's no requirement that the various parts play conventional progressions, such as the V-I progression shown in Figure 6-39. The term "bitonal" refers simply to a vertical sonority that employs two (or more) independent triads or extended chords.

Bitonal writing can become far more sophisticated than this. I'd encourage you to experiment with it on your own, and to listen to how bitonalism is used by composers like Aaron Copland.

You might expect that bitonality would be too weird or abstract to find a home in pop music — but in fact, bitonal chords are sometimes used in modern R&B. A chord chart that calls for ordinary 7th or 9th chords can sound too sweet or lacking in attitude. To create an edgier, more interesting sound, two chording instruments may play different chords, or the bass may imply one progression while a chording instrument plays a different progression.

There's no easy way to use chord symbols in bitonal writing. As noted in Chapter Five, a symbol like B♭/C usually indicates a B♭ major triad over a C bass note, not a B♭ major triad over a complete C major triad. If the element of the symbol that follows the slash mark contains a 7 or some other indication that a full chord is intended (for instance, B♭m9/C7), then it's clear that a complete bitonal voicing is being called for, not just a C bass note. But this type of symbol is hard to read, and in any case bitonality is seldom used in pop music chord charts, so you may never encounter such a chord symbol outside of a theory book.

## QUIZ

1. What term is used to describe a chord consisting of stacked 2nds?
2. What term is used to describe writing in which two instruments play different chords, or passages in different keys?
3. When the 3rd of a chord is replaced by a 4th, what is the chord called?
4. When a chord is described in a chord chart as an 11th, what other notes does it contain?
5. Why is there no such thing as a 15th chord?
6. What notes are contained in a Dmaj9? A B♭7♯11? An Em11? An F7♭9♯9?
7. What altered note is the same as the ♯11? What note would be the same as an aug13 (if there were such a thing as an aug13)?
8. What other chord contains the same notes as an E♭6? Describe the sound of a 6 chord.

# 7

# SCALES

---

**M**usic that consisted entirely of chord voicings would be interesting, but it wouldn't be very interesting for very long. Fortunately, there's more to music than chords. The framework provided by chordal harmonies can be expanded by adding extra notes — notes that are not part of the chord currently being played. These extra notes allow us to create music that's much more complex and expressive.

## NON-CHORD TONES

Take a look at Figure 7-1. While the left hand plays a C major triad, the right hand steps from one note to another. Three of the notes in this upper voice (the C, E, and G, which are circled in the figure) belong to the underlying C major chord. But the other two notes (D and F) are not found in the C major chord. These two notes are called *passing tones*, because the line played by the right hand uses them to pass from one chord tone to another.

Figure 7-2 is similar, but here the chord tones in the right-hand line are all E's, so we can't really say that the non-chord tones (F and D) are passing tones. When a voice leaves a chord tone in this manner, plays a nearby note, and then returns to the chord tone, the non-chord tone is said to be a *neighboring tone*. (The term *auxiliary tone* is also used.)

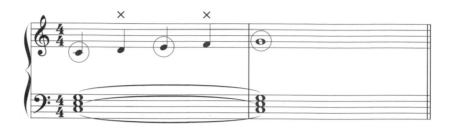

Figure 7-1. *The line in the treble clef includes both chord tones (circled) and non-chord tones (marked with X's). When a line uses non-chord tones to move from one chord tone to another, the non-chord tones are called* passing tones.

Figure 7-2. *Because the line in the treble clef moves away from and back to the same chord tone (E, circled), the non-chord tones (marked with X's) in the line are called* neighboring tones.

Both passing tones and neighboring tones are used in Figure 7-3. But in this example they're played above a chord progression. As a result, a note that's a passing tone in one measure, such as the D in measure 3, may be a chord tone in a different measure, such as in measure 2. This example also illustrates the fact that passing tones can connect the chord tones in two different chords. In measure 1, the B and A connect the C in the C chord with the G in the G chord. In measure 2, the F connects the G in the G chord with the E in the Am chord.

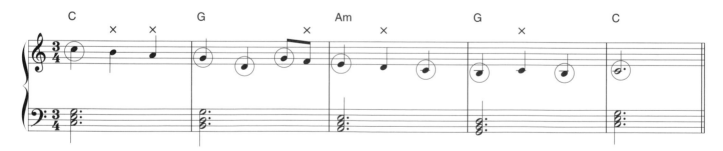

Figure 7-3. *Chord tones are circled and non-chord tones are marked with X's, as before. When a line is played over a chord progression, a note that's a chord tone in one measure can become a non-chord tone in another measure.*

Figure 7-4. The non-chord tones in this example (the B and C, marked with X's) are played at the same time as the chord (F major on beat 1, G major on beat 3), and then resolve downward to a chord tone. These non-chord tones are called suspensions or appoggiaturas.

A couple of other types of non-chord tones are worth mentioning before we go on. The *suspension,* also called an *appoggiatura,* was introduced in Chapter Six when we talked about suspended chords. The suspension is a non-chord tone that's played at the beginning of the chord. It then moves either up or down to a neighboring chord tone, as shown in Figure 7-4.

In passing, we should note that in Baroque classical music, the term "appoggiatura" has a more specialized meaning. While it sounds and functions exactly as we've just described, it's written with a small notehead, as if it were a grace note, but with no slash-mark through the stem. Beginning around 1800, composers stopped writing appoggiaturas as if they were ornaments, but continued to use them pretty much as they had been used before. In this book, the word is used in the more modern sense.

If the suspended note never resolves by moving up or down to a chord tone, we're dealing with a suspended chord type, in which case the suspended note would be a chord tone within a different chord, not a non-chord tone. (For classical theorists, the suspension is always a non-chord tone, even if it never resolves. But this is not the case in popular music, where suspended chords are felt to stand on their own.) In the discussion in this chapter, we'll assume that the chord type is a simple triad or 7th chord, and that the suspended note resolves to a chord tone.

Figure 7-5. In the upper line in this example, chord tones are played before the beat on which the chord itself is played. Thus each of these notes starts out as a non-chord tone (for instance, the D on beat 2 of bar 1, which is a non-chord tone in relation to the C major chord). These non-chord tones are called anticipations, because they anticipate the chord that's about to be played.

In a suspension, the chord tone in the moving voice arrives *after* the rest of the chord. If a chord tone of a given chord is instead played early, while the previous chord is still playing, and if this note is not part of the previous chord, it's called an *anticipation*. The upper voice in Figure 7-5 plays a series of anticipations. Each note in this voice after the first note anticipates the following chord: The D on beat 2 of measure 1 anticipates the G major triad that arrives on beat 3, the C on beat 4 of measure 1 anticipates the F major triad that arrives in measure 2, and so on. With respect to the C chord in measure 1, the D is a non-chord tone.

Non-chord tones can be deployed in a line in other ways; the discussion in this section is not exhaustive by any means. Consider the possibilities in Figure 7-6, for instance. The point of introducing the concept of non-chord tones is to give you some ideas about how to use scales, to which we'll turn next.

Figure 7-6. Non-chord tones can be used in more elaborate ways. In measure 1 here, the upper line starts on a non-chord tone, moves past the chord tone to another non-chord tone, and finally lands on the chord tone. The B here is called an escape tone, *because the melodic line starts with a D appoggiatura and then "escapes" past the expected resolution on the C before returning. In the second measure, the first non-chord tone (E) is embellished with its own neighboring tone, after which the E and C♯ (both non-chord tones) alternate before the D chord tone arrives.*

Non-chord tones add dissonance to the harmony, and dissonance creates tension. When the non-chord tone resolves to a chord tone, the tension disappears. This fact is what makes non-chord tones so important. By deploying passing tones, neighboring tones, suspensions, and anticipations, composers create harmonic passages that are filled with emotional meaning.

The terminology used to describe non-chord tones may seem a bit academic. I can't recall ever hearing a pop songwriter talk about using an appoggiatura or an anticipation. But such devices are used all the time. And not just in melodies. Figure 7-7 shows a funk-type rhythm comp that contains a two-note appoggiatura (the two inner notes on beat 1 of bar 1), neighboring tones (the same two inner notes, when repeated on the second beat), and an anticipation (the E and B♭ at the end of bar 1, which anticipate the C9 chord in bar 2).

Sometimes it's a matter of personal preference whether to analyze a given note as a non-chord tone, or whether to look at it as changing the chord type. If

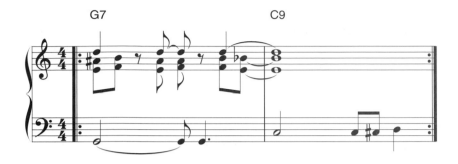

*Figure 7-7. The two inner notes on the first beat of measure 1 are suspended notes (appoggiaturas) leading into the chord tones F and B from below. The E and B♭ at the end of measure 1 are anticipations, because they arrive before the C9 chord. The C♯ and D in the bass line at the end of measure 2, however, don't quite fit any of the designations used in the text to describe non-chord tones. If we consider the D the root of an implied D7 chord (the dominant of G), then the C♯ is a passing tone.*

the harmonic context provided by surrounding chords consists mostly of triads, then it would complicate matters needlessly to start talking about added 9ths and 11ths. The bass line in Figure 7-8 provides a good example of this. On beat 2 of measure 1, the B in the bass effectively turns the C major triad into a Cmaj7 chord in third inversion. Likewise, the Am triad in the second half of the bar becomes an Am7 in third inversion when the bass line moves down to G. In a folk music or country music setting, where a songwriter or arranger would rarely call for a maj7 or m7 chord type, calling the B and G passing tones makes a lot more sense.

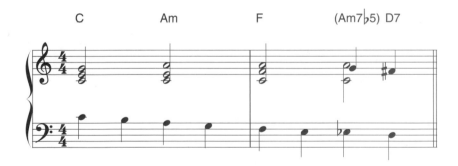

*Figure 7-8. The passing tones in the bass line (B, G, and E) turn the triads into 7th chords in third inversion (Cmaj7, Am7, and Fmaj7, respectively). Most arrangers wouldn't bother inserting new chord symbols on the beats where these notes are played, however. The double appoggiatura on the D7 chord is more debatable. I wrote it this way because I liked the sound, and the underlying progression is clearly moving from F to D7, but if you'd prefer to call the chord on beat 3 of bar 2 an Am7♭5 leading to a D7 on beat 4, I won't argue with you.*

## THE MAJOR SCALE

Now that you know a few ways to deploy non-chord tones, the question that naturally arises is, how do you know which notes to choose? While any note in the chromatic scale is fair game for a non-chord tone, most often you'll choose notes drawn from the current scale.

The major scale, which was introduced in Chapter Two, is not the only scale used in European and American music by any means, but it's the most important one. In Chapter Three, we used the notes of the major scale to build triads. The idea that most music is in a key was also introduced. The relationship between the key and the major scale is of central importance. If a piece is in the key of D major, for instance, it will use (most of the time) both chords and non-chord tones drawn from the D major scale.

The major scale (see Figure 7-9) contains a pattern of whole-steps and half-steps. Starting on the note that's the tonic of the scale, the scale contains two whole-steps followed by a half-step, and then three more whole-steps followed by another half-step. It's this pattern — W-W-H, then W-W-W-H — that constitutes the major scale.

The white keys on the keyboard form a major scale in the key of C. When you play a major scale in a different key, you'll need to use some black keys so as to get the same pattern of whole-steps and half-steps. Almost anybody can play a C major scale (a cat walking on the keyboard can do it), but learning the patterns of white and black keys that form the other major scales may take a little effort, at least when you're new to playing the keyboard.

Other patterns of whole-steps and half-steps can be used to make other types of scales. Some of these are closely related to the major scale, while others are more distantly related. In the remainder of this chapter, we'll explore various ways to construct scales, and show how they can be used in conjunction with chords.

## THE GREEK MODES

Starting with the major scale, we can generate six new scales simply by choosing a different note for the tonic. The usual term for the scales created in this way is *modes.* Several of the modes are often used in improvisation, so it's important to

*Figure 7-9. One octave of a C major scale. The whole-steps are marked with square brackets, the half-steps with angled brackets. This pattern of whole-steps and half-steps is repeated in all of the major scales.*

understand them. They're shown in Figure 7-10, and again in Figure 7-11. Table 7-1 provides the same information as Figures 7-10 and 7-11; some musicians may find the concept easier to grasp when it's presented in tabular form.

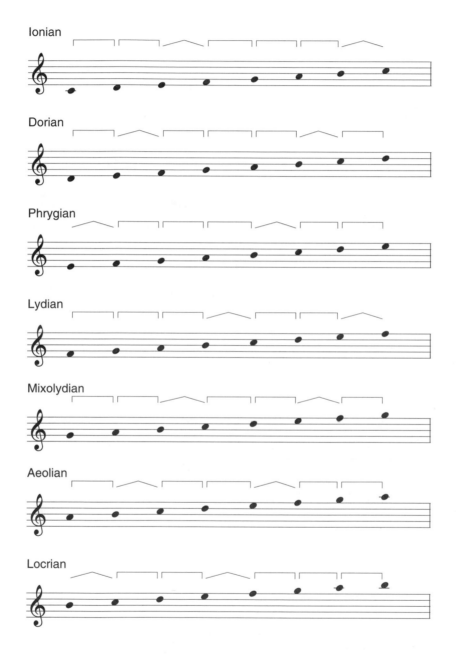

*Figure 7-10. By using the same set of whole-steps and half-steps that are found in the major scale, but starting and ending on a different tonic note, we can generate seven different melodic modes. The Ionian mode (which is the same as the major scale) starts and ends on C, the Dorian mode on D, the Phrygian mode on E, the Lydian mode on F, the Mixolydian mode on G, the Aeolian mode on A, and the Locrian mode on B.*

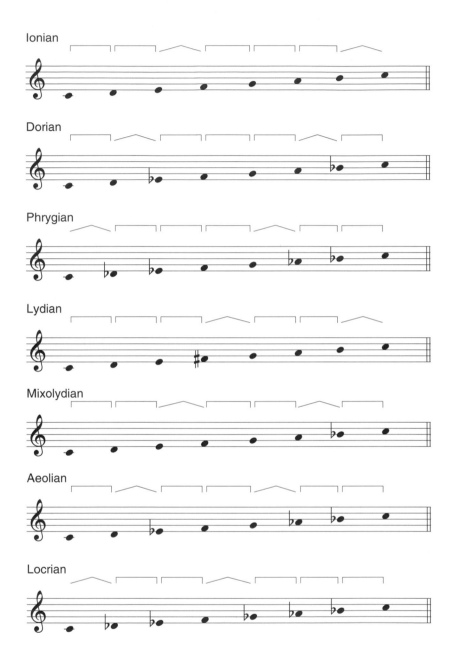

*Figure 7-11. Here, the seven modes shown in Figure 7-10 have been transposed so that they all start and end on C (the tonic). The pattern of whole-steps and half-steps is marked as before, with square brackets for whole-steps and angled brackets for half-steps.*

| Mode | Arrangement of steps | Tonic when mode is played on white keys | Key signature when tonic is C |
|---|---|---|---|
| Ionian | W-W-H-W-W-W-H | C | no flats or sharps |
| Dorian | W-H-W-W-W-H-W | D | 2 flats |
| Phrygian | H-W-W-W-H-W-W | E | 4 flats |
| Lydian | W-W-W-H-W-W-H | F | 1 sharp |
| Mixolydian | W-W-H-W-W-H-W | G | 1 flat |
| Aeolian | W-H-W-W-H-W-W | A | 3 flats |
| Locrian | H-W-W-H-W-W-W | B | 5 flats |

*Table 7-1. The Greek modes.*

The term "mode" means something like "manner" or "method." It's a way of saying that we're doing the same thing we were doing before, only in a different way. In this case, we're using the arrangement of whole-steps and half-steps found in the major scale — two whole-steps and then a half-step, followed by three whole-steps and a half-step — but we're calling a different note the tonic. Or, to look at it a different way, we're sliding the half-steps to the left or right so that they fall in a different spot in relation to the tonic. The major scale, which is also called the Ionian mode, starts with two whole-steps. If we consider D the tonic rather than C, the mode starts with one whole-step followed by a half-step, then three more whole-steps and so on. This is called the Dorian mode. The next mode, Phrygian, runs from E up to E on the white keys of the keyboard, so it begins with a half-step. Note that this mode is quite different from the E major scale, because the latter uses four black keys (F♯, G♯, C♯, and D♯), while the E Phrygian mode uses only white keys.

Our ears are so used to hearing the major scale that if you simply start playing the white keys on the keyboard, before long your ear will probably tell you you're playing in C major, no matter what note you try to hear as the tonic. It may be difficult to hear the Dorian mode or any of the other modes as a distinct entity. Hearing them will get easier when we start playing them in combination with chords.

Most of the names of the modes originated during the Medieval period; others were added later. While Medieval music theorists were fond of using terminology drawn from ancient sources, the modes have very little relationship to the music played in ancient Greece. The Greeks gave similar names to some of their scales, but we have very little idea what those scales actually sounded like. The modes used in Medieval church music were somewhat different from the modern modes with the same names, and are of interest only to musicologists, so unless you're working toward a music degree there's no reason for you to clutter your brain with them.

## USING MODES WITH CHORDS

An important reason why modes are important is because they give us a repertoire of scales that can be used easily in conjunction with specific types of 7th chord. To see how this works, play the music in Figure 7-12. To begin with, the scale in measure 1 obviously works with the D7 chord: It contains all of the notes in the chord. Now figure out where the whole-steps and half-steps are in the scale

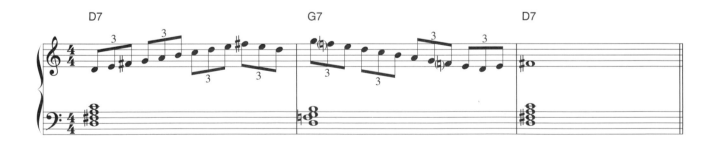

Figure 7-12. Since blues progressions often use a dominant 7th chord as the I, this D7-G7 progression is most likely a I7-IV7 progression in the key of D. Over each of the 7th chords, a soloist can play in Mixolydian mode. The scale shown above the D7 is D Mixolydian, and the scale above the G7 is G Mixolydian.

used in measure 1. Since this scale has one sharp, you can probably see at a glance that it must be a G major scale (Ionian mode with a tonic note of G). But in the heat of improvisation, trying to remember that you need to play a G major scale over a D7 chord is likely to be a bit confusing. If you look at this scale as a mode whose tonic note is D (the same note as the root of the underlying chord), you'll discover that you're looking at D Mixolydian.

As Figure 7-11 shows, Mixolydian mode has the same structure as a major scale, except that the 7th step (the leading tone) is lowered. This lowered step corresponds to the minor 7th in a dominant 7th chord (C♮ above the D root). So Figure 7-12 illustrates the first concept in applying modes:

> Over an unaltered dominant 7th or dominant 9th chord, use the Mixolydian mode whose tonic is the same as the root of the chord.

The same thing happens in measure 2 of Figure 7-12. The chord, G7, is an unaltered dominant, so the scale to play over it is G Mixolydian. This figure illustrates another important concept as well: In many types of pop music, but especially jazz and blues, the scale or mode from which melody notes are drawn is quite likely to change when the chord changes. Experienced improvisers learn a variety of modes and scales in all 12 keys, so as to be able to switch from one to another fluidly.

When analyzing which mode is used in a melodic line, it's important to understand that the note on which the line starts (or ends) doesn't matter. To make it easier for you to see that the modes used in Figure 7-12 are Mixolydian, I arranged the music in such a way that the right-hand line in each measure started on the tonic note of the mode. But this is not necessary. A line can start or end on any note of the mode. Also, Figure 7-12 is written so that the right-hand line in each measure moves in a scalewise fashion, one step at a time. In real-world soloing, it would be the exception rather than the rule that a line would do this for an entire measure. In most types of classical music, running up or down a scale is stylistically appropriate, but in jazz and pop, straight scales tend to sound quite square and stiff. Many of the lines shown in this chapter are intentionally kept very simple, so that they'll be easier for you to analyze.

Now look at Figure 7-13. The chord in the first two measures is a minor 7th. If we assume that the mode of the notes in the right hand has the same tonic (E) as the root of the Em7 chord, by analyzing the pattern of whole-steps and half-steps you'll be able to see that this line is in E Dorian mode. Whenever you see an unaltered minor 7th chord, you can play in the Dorian mode whose tonic is the same as the root of the chord.

Measures 3 and 4 of the same passage call for a dominant 7th chord whose root is A. (Most likely, we're looking at a IIm7-V7 progression in the key of D.) The

*Figure 7-13. Above a minor 7th chord, you can use the Dorian mode. In this example, E Dorian is used above the Em7. Above the A7, A Mixolydian is used, as in Figure 7-12. Note that E Dorian and A Mixolydian share all of the same notes.*

mode used above the A7 is A Mixolydian, as explained above. If you examine the right-hand line in this figure, however, you'll see that the scale, which contains two sharps, doesn't change when the chord changes. This fact points out another important concept:

> Over a IIm7-V7 progression, use the Dorian mode over the IIm7 and the Mixolydian over the V7. Because of the relationship between the chord roots, the two modes will contain exactly the same notes.

The Ionian mode (the major scale) is used whenever the chord is an unaltered major 7th type. Measure 2 in Figure 7-14 shows this. Here again, the E♭ Ionian mode has the same underlying scale steps as the F Dorian and B♭ Mixolydian. In real-world progressions, however, you can't necessarily assume that you'll be playing in the same scale (and calling it by a different name) when the chord changes. Figure 7-15 shows what happens to the progression in Figure 7-14 when we use a tritone substitution in place of the V7 chord. The notes in measure 2 are drawn from the E Mixolydian mode, which is utterly different from the B♭ Mixolydian

*Figure 7-14. Above a major 7th chord, such as the E♭maj7 in measure 2, you can use notes from the Ionian mode.*

*Figure 7-15. Some chord changes require that the mode used for the melody change drastically from measure to measure. Here, F Dorian in measure 1 is followed by E Mixolydian in measure 2.*

used in Figure 7-14. In fact, these two modes have only two notes in common: D and G♯/A♭. These two notes are the major 3rd and minor 7th of the two dominant-type chords.

If you've looked closely at Figures 7-14 and 7-15, you may be wondering why in both of them I skipped the 4th scale step of the Ionian mode over the major 7th chord. Depending on the harmonic context, this note may not sound very good, so it's sometimes skipped. Some other modes have notes that can clash with the underlying harmony: Musicians often skip the 4th step when playing in the Mixolydian mode and the 6th step when playing in the Dorian mode. Figure 7-16 shows these modes as they might be employed by a soloist. Other alterations in the modes are possible; we'll look at a few of them later in this chapter.

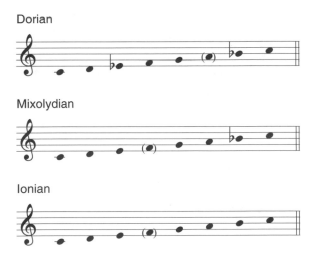

*Figure 7-16. When drawing melody notes from a mode, it's not necessary to use all of the notes of the mode. The 6th step is often skipped in Dorian mode, and the 4th step is often skipped in Mixolydian and Ionian.*

Speaking of scale notes that don't sound good, I've noticed that many guitarists have a bad habit of using the Dorian mode when soloing in a minor key — that is, the Dorian whose root is the tonic of the key — even when the chords they're soloing over include a minor IV or a major triad on the ♭VI. Since the Dorian has a raised 6th step (A♮ in the key of C), while these two triads use a lowered 6th step (A♭ in the key of C), Aeolian mode might be a better choice. Some guitarists may employ this harmonic clash deliberately to heighten tension, but I'm fairly sure a lot of them do it because they're not paying enough attention to which modes fit with which chords.

The Lydian, Phrygian, and Locrian modes are used less frequently in pop and jazz music, but they're worth knowing about. The Locrian mode can be used over a m7♭5 chord, as shown in Figure 7-17. Lydian is used over a major9♯11, as shown in Figure 7-18, or over a IVmaj7. Phrygian is seldom used in its unaltered form, because the flat 2nd and 3rd steps give it a somewhat foreign sound. Aeolian may or may not be used for soloing and melodies, depending on how you look at it: If the 6th step of the mode is left out, as it would usually be, Aeolian is the same as Dorian (see Figure 7-16). Aeolian is important for another reason, however: It's better known as the natural minor scale.

Figure 7-17. Over the Em7♭5 in measure 1, the right-hand line uses the E Locrian mode.

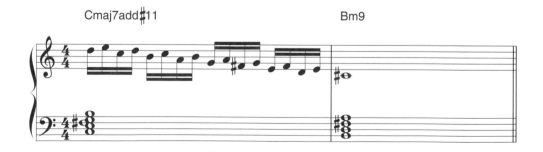

Figure 7-18. Over a major 7th chord with a sharp 11th, the Lydian mode works well.

## MINOR SCALES

The concept of minor keys was introduced in Chapter Four. Each major key, you'll recall, has a relative minor key. The relative minor has the same key signature as its relative major, and its tonic is a minor 3rd below the tonic of the major. If you surmise from this description and from Figure 7-10 that the basic scale of a minor key is the Aeolian mode, you'd be right. Figure 7-19 shows the relationship. C major is the relative major of A minor (and A minor is the relative minor of C major). The Aeolian mode whose tonic is A has the same notes as the Ionian mode whose tonic is C.

As was explained briefly in Chapter Four, however, the V triad in a minor key is sometimes altered from minor to major in order to provide a more satisfying harmonic movement. When this triad is altered, its 3rd, which is the 7th step of the minor scale, is raised. In addition, the 6th step of the scale is sometimes raised. As a result, the minor scale has some significant variations that the major scale lacks.

The Aeolian mode is called the *natural minor scale*, because neither its 6th nor its 7th step is altered. (This term has nothing to do with whether the 6th and 7th steps are spelled with naturals or flats. It simply indicates that the scale is in its natural, unaltered state.) When the major V triad or dominant V7 chord is used, the 7th note of the scale (the 3rd of the V chord) is raised by a half-step. This scale, which is shown in Figure 7-20, is called the *harmonic minor scale*, because the leading tone has been raised to coincide with the harmony (the major V triad). The harmonic minor scale sounds faintly odd or exotic to our ears, because it contains an augmented 2nd interval. In fact, it sounds odd enough that composers often prefer to avoid it. They do this by raising the 6th step of the scale whenever it's being used before a raised 7th.

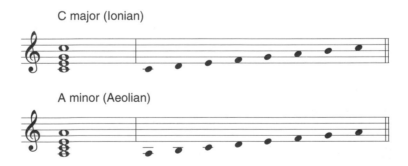

*Figure 7-19. The key of A minor is the relative minor of C major, and C major is the relative major of C minor. An interval of a minor 3rd separates the roots of any relative major and its relative minor. The relative minor uses the Aeolian mode as its scale.*

Figure 7-20. The harmonic minor scale contains an augmented 2nd interval (from F to G♯ in the A harmonic minor scale).

In classical music of the 18th and 19th centuries, the norm was to write melodies in such a way that both the 6th and 7th steps of the minor scale were raised — but only when the melody was moving upward. The raised leading tone would be preceded by a raised 6th step: As a result, the upper half of the minor scale would be the same as the upper half of a major scale. Only the lowered 3rd step would indicate that the scale was minor. When the melody was moving downward, however, the natural minor scale would most often be used instead. This practice, which is illustrated in Figure 7-21, is not followed in any rigorous way by modern composers, but it gave rise to the terminology used to describe these scales. A minor scale in which both the 6th and 7th steps have been raised is called the *ascending melodic minor scale*. Sorry, sports fans — it's a bloated, clumsy term, but we're stuck with it. The descending melodic minor scale is the same as the natural minor scale, so the term "descending melodic minor" is used less often.

The ascending melodic minor turns out to be an interesting scale in its own right. As shown in Figure 7-22, it has a different pattern of whole-steps and half-steps than any of the modes discussed above. Compare Figure 7-21 to Figure 7-11:

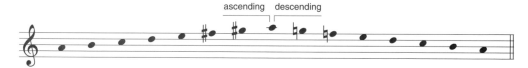

Figure 7-21. The melodic minor scale has two forms. When the line is moving upward, the 6th and 7th steps are raised, but when the line is moving downward, they're not raised.

Figure 7-22. The ascending melodic minor scale in C. This scale has a different pattern of whole-steps and half-steps. It also contains an interval of an augmented 5th (between the 3rd and 7th steps, which here are E♭ and B). This interval is not found in any of the major scale modes.

None of the modes in Figure 7-11 has four whole-steps in a row. Their whole-steps are all in a 3/2 pattern.

This fact might suggest to you that we can generate a whole new set of modes by performing the same type of transformation on the ascending melodic minor scale that we performed on the major scale. In fact, this is an eminently feasible procedure. While the modes created in this way, which are shown in Figure 7-23, don't have names, some of them are quite useful in conjunction with certain of the altered chords introduced in Chapter Six.

Figure 7-23. The ascending melodic minor can be played in seven different modes. The fourth mode shown here, containing a raised 4th and a lowered 7th, was used by 20th-century composer Béla Bartók, and is sometimes referred to as "the Bartók scale." The enharmonic spelling of the steps in the last mode is somewhat arbitrary. It could be notated as C, D♭, E♭, F♭, G♭, A♭, B♭, C, but reading an F♭ in sheet music isn't easy — besides which, this note is functionally the 3rd of a major triad, so why spell it as if it were the 4th?

To figure out which mode might be useful with which chord, simply play the chord and then fill in the steps between the chord tones with non-chord tones of one sort or another. At the level where we're operating now, there are no right or wrong choices: It's pretty much up to you to find a mode that you like the sound of. A few options to get you started are shown in Figure 7-24.

Figure 7-24. The modes derived from the ascending melodic minor scale can be used for constructing melodies over certain altered chords. Here are five of the more useful possibilities. If you're a keyboard player, try sustaining each of the chords shown in your left hand while improvising over it in the right hand using the mode shown.

## CHROMATIC SPELLING

When writing out a passage, especially when it has a number of sharps or flats in the key signature, it's sometimes a bit of a puzzle how to spell a given note. The general rule is that when a line is ascending, accidentals that raise the pitch should be used. When a line is descending, the chromatic spelling should use accidentals that lower the pitch.

There are two reasons for this. First, it's a good idea to spell a scale with consecutive letter-names when possible. For instance, B-C#-D#-E is preferable to

B-D♭-E♭-E♮, even though both spellings contain the same pitches, because B-C-D-E is a sensible scale fragment, while B-D-E-E has a skip (from B to D) and a repetition (two E's) in it. The second reason is because when you do it this way, the sheet music will generally require fewer accidentals. Assuming the key signature is C major (no sharps or flats), the line B-C♯-D♯-E will have two accidentals in it, while B-D♭-E♭-E♮ has three because the flat before the first E has to be cancelled. Figure 7-25 illustrates both of these points.

*Figure 7-25. The enharmonic spelling in (a) is preferable to the one in (b), because the motion through a scale by step is clearer, and because fewer accidentals are needed.*

This particular scale fragment, which is probably either the lower half of a B major scale or the upper half of an E major scale, would usually be spelled the same whether it was ascending or descending. But if we replace the B with a C♮ and then apply the same rules, the simplest spelling will be C-C♯-D♯-E if we're ascending and E-E♭-D♭-C if we're descending, as shown in Figure 7-26. In each case, we have a scale fragment (C-D-E or E-D-C) with one repeated letter-name at the beginning. The number of accidentals is kept to a minimum, and the accidentals indicate the direction of the line.

The actual spelling used will, however, be affected by two other factors: the key signature and the harmonic meaning of the individual notes. If the key sig-

*Figure 7-26. The choice of whether to spell notes enharmonically as sharps or flats often depends on which direction the line is moving. Sharps are more appropriate for ascending lines, and flats for descending lines, because fewer accidentals are needed. The spellings shown in (a) and (b) are preferable to those shown in (c) and (d).*

nature is four flats (A♭ major), this line would normally be spelled C-D♭-E♭-E♮ even when it's ascending. No accidentals would be needed before the D and E, because they're already flatted in the key signature, so the line could be written with only one accidental (E♮). Using sharps in such a case would violate the rule that the number of accidentals should be kept to a minimum. Conversely, if the key signature has four sharps, the descending line would be spelled either E-D♯-C♯-C♮ or E-D♯-C♯-B♯. In either case, only one accidental (before the last note) would have to be printed. Whether the last note is spelled C♮ or B♯ depends partly on its harmonic meaning. Lacking any other information except the key signature (four sharps), it would be spelled as a B♯ when the line is ascending, and as a C♮ when it's descending, as shown in Figure 7-27. If it's part of a G♯7 chord (a V7 of VI in E), it would definitely be spelled as a B♯. If it's part of a D7, on the other hand (which is rather far afield in the key of E, but which would be right at home in a jazz chart), it would be spelled as a C♮. These spellings would be used no matter which direction the line was moving.

*Figure 7-27. The presence of a key signature will sometimes affect how notes in a scale are spelled. The chromatic pitches in this example are the same as those in Figure 7-26, but the spelling will be mostly the same whether the line is ascending or descending.*

When these rules are applied systematically, notes will occasionally have to be spelled using double-sharps and double-flats, as Figure 7-28 illustrates. Double-sharped and double-flatted notes are hard to sight-read, but keeping the written music theoretically clear usually makes it worthwhile to put up with a bit of awkwardness in reading. On the other hand, there are situations where it's almost a coin-toss how to spell a note within a chord. A classic case is the so-called "German sixth" chord, which we'll meet in Chapter Eight. In 18th- and 19th-century classical music, this chord was normally spelled with an augmented sixth, as shown in Figure 7-29, because the top note resolved by moving upward chromatically. (By the same argument, the 5th of the chord should have been spelled as a

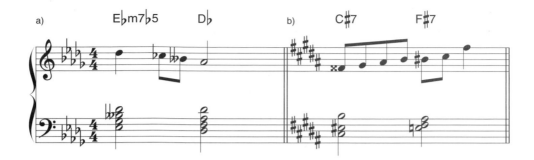

*Figure 7-28. In order to use the correct enharmonic spelling of notes in keys that have lots of flats or sharps in the key signature, sheet music occasionally has to resort to double-flats or double-sharps. The A♭♭ in (a) makes both the spelling of the scale fragment (D-C-B-A) and the 7th chord (E-G-B-D) clear. The F✗ in (b) could perhaps be spelled as a G♮ (which would be the flat 5th of the C♯7 chord), but the melody can be notated with fewer accidentals when a double-sharp is used. The same argument applies to the B♯, by the way.*

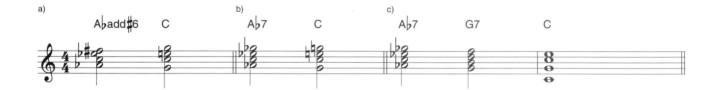

*Figure 7-29. The traditional spelling of the dominant-type chord in this progression (a) makes more sense in terms of the chromatic upward movement of the top voice. But the spelling in (b), which makes the chord easier to read, tends to be preferred by musicians today. Perhaps this is because the chord is just as likely to resolve downward, as shown in (c). A pre-20th-century classical composer would have been unlikely to use this resolution, because of the parallel 5ths.*

doubly augmented 4th — but never mind.) The fact that this chord has the same structure as an ordinary dominant 7th, however, means that the augmented 6th is more naturally spelled as a minor 7th. When it's spelled this way, an extra accidental is needed in the music, as Figure 7-29 makes clear. Even so, the fact that it's easier to read the chord, in combination with the fact that the chord isn't part of the diatonic structure of the key in the first place, has led musicians often to prefer the easier spelling.

# THE WHOLE-TONE SCALE

There's no law that says scales always have to have exactly two half-steps. If we eliminate half-steps entirely, the result is the *whole-tone scale* (see Figure 7-30). This scale contains only whole-steps. The whole-tone scale is symmetrical with respect to the tonic. With the major and ascending melodic minor modes, when we choose a different tonic note to start and end on, the sound of the scale changes. But no matter which note of a whole-tone scale we start and end on, the scale sounds exactly the same.

Because the chromatic scale contains 12 tones while each whole-tone scale contains six, there are only two whole-tone scales. This fact is a boon to instrumentalists: They only have to learn two fingerings to be able to play whole-tone scales in all 12 keys.

The whole-tone scale is ideal for playing above 7♭5 and 7♯5 chords, as Figure 7-31 shows. All of the chord tones are found in the scale.

*Figure 7-30. The two whole-tone scales. These scales have to be written using a diminished 3rd interval, but all of the steps are the same size.*

*Figure 7-31. A whole-tone scale works well for melodies above a dominant chord containing a ♯5 or ♭5 (or both).*

## THE DIMINISHED SCALE

Another symmetrical scale is known as the *diminished scale* (see Figure 7-32). It gets its name from the fact that it's constructed using all of the notes of two different diminished 7th chords. There are exactly three diminished scales in all, a fact you should verify for yourself by picking them out on the keyboard. As with diminished 7th chords, each scale has four notes that can be looked at interchangeably as the root.

We can look at a diminished scale as starting with either a half-step or a whole-step. The former turns out to be more useful when this scale is being used for soloing. Over the dominant 7th chord shown in Figure 7-33, voiced in a standard way with no 5th, all of the steps of the diminished scale can easily be heard as chord tones.

Figure 7-32. There are three diminished scales. Each contains the same pattern of alternating whole-steps and half-steps.

Figure 7-33. If we consider the diminished scale as starting with a half-step, all of the notes in the scale are chord tones above a dominant 7th chord with no 5th.

The diminished scale also contains major triads, but to get them, we have to skip a scale step. In the scale in Figure 7-33, for instance, the first, fourth, and sixth steps outline the C major triad implied by the left-hand chord. Figure 7-34 shows the major triads in this scale. If you're interested in bitonal music or progressions with ambiguous tonal centers, you might find this progression worth playing around with.

*Figure 7-34. If we consider a diatonic triad as containing the root, 3rd, and 5th steps of the scale (or the 2nd, 4th, and 6th steps, or whatever), all of the diatonic triads of a diminished scale are diminished. Even so, the scale contains four major triads. Shown here are the major triads found in the C diminished scale in Figure 7-33.*

## PENTATONIC SCALES

The major and ascending melodic minor modes are all seven-note scales. The whole-tone scale has only six notes, while the diminished scale has eight notes. Another useful group of scales contains only five notes per scale. These scales are known collectively as *pentatonic scales*. ("Penta-" is a Greek prefix that means "five.") Since there are 12 notes in the chromatic scale, you might expect that we could construct quite a variety of scales by choosing five of the notes at a time. Only a few pentatonic scales are in common use, however.

The most important are the major and minor pentatonic scales, which are shown in Figure 7-35. These scales contain no half-steps, only whole-steps and minor thirds. In fact, they both have the same underlying pattern of whole-steps and minor thirds (W-W-M linked to W-M). As a result, it's easy to see that the C minor pentatonic contains the same notes as the E♭ major pentatonic.

*Figure 7-35. The major pentatonic and minor pentatonic scales (left and right, respectively). These scales contain minor 3rds, which are marked with a V. I've placed the upper tonic note in parentheses to remind you that the reason these scales are called pentatonic is because they contain five different tones. The sixth note is the octave.*

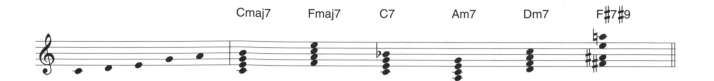

Figure 7-36. The C major pentatonic can be used for soloing above any of the chords shown here. Okay, maybe the F#7#9 is a stretch, but a jazz soloist wouldn't have a problem with it. As an exercise, you should work out the harmonic function of each of the notes in the scale with reference to each chord root. Above the Dm7, for instance, the G in the scale is an added 4th.

Playing an F# major or D# minor pentatonic scale on the keyboard is easy: Just play the black keys.

Pentatonic scales of this type are often used for soloing, because a single scale will work above more than one chord. A few possibilities are shown in Figure 7-36. As you can see from this figure, the C major pentatonic is compatible with both Cmaj7 and C7 chords.

Other pentatonic scales are used in musical traditions from Asia and Africa. Since these traditions don't use equal-tempered tuning, they can only be approximated by Western instruments, but they can give your music an exotic flavor that you may find worth cultivating. A couple of non-Western pentatonics are shown in Figure 7-37. When using these scales, it may be a good idea to avoid non-scale tones: As you add other notes, the pentatonics will start to sound like conventional Western modes.

Figure 7-37. These pentatonic scales are used more often in music of Asia and Africa than in Western music, but they're worth experimenting with. Try improvising a short piece using one of them without adding any non-scale tones.

Figure 7-38. An altered Phrygian mode in which the 3rd has been raised.

Earlier I noted that the Phrygian mode is seldom used in an unaltered form. But the second pentatonic scale shown in Figure 7-37 has the same lowered 2nd as the Phrygian. It also has an exotic-sounding augmented 2nd interval. Combining the two scales, we might come up with a scale like the one in Figure 7-38. If this scale has a name, I've never learned it, but it's quite useful in one specific instance: for soloing over the classic Spanish/flamenco progression shown in Figure 7-39. This works because the scale contains major triads on both the I and ♭II.

*Figure 7-39. The scale in Figure 7-38 can be used for soloing over a I-♭II progression. This scale could be further altered, depending on the desired musical effect, by raising the 7th step so that it can function better as a leading tone. In addition, a lowered 3rd (G♮ in the key of E) could be inserted between the 2nd and the major 3rd.*

## THE BLUES SCALE

The musical genre known as the blues developed in the early 20th century. Because its origins lie in the African-American communities of the Southern U.S., certain of the harmonic devices employed in the blues are probably descended from the indigenous folk music traditions of West Africa. Irrespective of where the blues came from, it has profoundly influenced American culture: The blues tradition gave birth both to early jazz and to early rock and roll. At the same time, blues music has remained a vital genre in its own right.

In Chapter Eight, we'll take a look at the standard chord progressions used in the blues. But no chapter on scales would be complete without a discussion of the blues scale.

In its simplest form, the blues scale has the same form as the minor pentatonic. What makes this scale interesting is that when the blues chord progression changes from the I chord to the IV and the V, the scale doesn't change. Thus the notes of the scale have different harmonic implications, depending on which chord they're played with. Figure 7-40 illustrates this idea.

The minor pentatonic is often enriched with some extra notes, which are generally used as passing tones or appoggiaturas. The most frequently used extra tones are shown in Figure 7-41. Since the scale in 7-41b contains nine of the 12

Swing eighths

*Figure 7-40. A 12-bar blues chorus in D (omitting the last two bars). All of the notes in this rather stiff but reasonably idiomatic blues melody are drawn from the D pentatonic minor scale. This results in some harmonic clashes that are characteristic of the blues. First, the augmented 9ths — or, if you prefer, minor 3rds — of the I and V triads are included in the scale: An F♮ is played above the F♯ in the D7 chord, and a C♮ above the C♯ in the A7 chord. Second, the 4th is used freely above all three chords (G above the D7 chord, C above the G7 chord, and D above the A7 chord), which clashes with the major 3rd. Finally, above the A7 chord the F♮ is a ♯5.*

notes in the chromatic scale, you might easily assume that in the blues scale almost any note can be used at any time. What's essential to understand about this extended form of the blues scale is that all of the notes are *not* created equal. Unlike a scale in classical music, the extended blues scale is never played by simply running up and down the scale. It's an *inflected* scale, which is a fancy way of saying that certain notes have particular relationships to other notes.

a)

b)

*Figure 7-41. The pentatonic blues scale in Figure 7-40 can be expanded by adding the flat 5th, as seen in (a) here. This note is highly unstable harmonically, and always resolves either upward to the natural 5th or downward to the 4th. Whether it's spelled enharmonically as a sharp 4th or a flat 5th is a matter of taste. A more complete version of the blues scale is shown in (b). The major 3rd has been added, as have the two notes shown in parentheses. These notes most often function as secondary tones that resolve upward or downward. The minor 3rd (E♭ in the key of C, as shown here) can be used either as a secondary tone tending upward to the major 3rd, or on its own. If the chord progression uses a minor I chord, the major 3rd will be avoided.*

Swing eighths

*Figure 7-42. The sharp 4th in the blues scale (which can just as easily be notated as a flat 5th) is unstable, and resolves either upward to the 5th or downward to the 4th. This lick shows both types of resolution.*

The sharp 4th step, for instance, is almost always followed by the natural 4th or the natural 5th. It's an unstable note, and has to resolve either upward or downward, as in the blues lick in Figure 7-42. In the same way, the 2nd usually resolves upward to the minor 3rd or downward to the root, and the 6th resolves upward to the minor 7th or downward to the 5th. A lick that illustrates these uses of the 6th and 2nd is shown in Figure 7-43.

If the major 3rd is used at all, the minor 3rd will probably be treated in the same way, as an unstable tone that resolves upward to the major 3rd. Above the IV7 chord, however, the major 3rd of the scale would usually be avoided, because it would clash with the minor 7th of the IV chord.

*Figure 7-43. Like the ♯4/♭5, the 2nd and 6th of the blues scale are secondary tones, and usually resolve to higher or lower tones.*

The use of grace-notes in Figures 7-42 and 7-43 is typical of blues played on a piano. Guitarists and singers, however, and keyboardists who play synthesizers, can *bend* notes up or down, gliding smoothly from one tone in the equal-tempered scale to another. (Technically, a guitarist can only bend notes upward, but by picking the note after bending a string sharp and then letting the string fall back to its original fretted pitch, the guitarist can create the illusion of a downward bend.) Bending notes is an essential part of blues technique. Both the secondary notes shown in parentheses in Figure 7-41 and the main notes above and below them are often produced by bending.

Blues bends don't always change the pitch by an equal-tempered half-step. Sometimes a bend takes a while to move from one pitch to another, and the note may end before the nominal destination is reached — or the bend may fall back to a lower pitch without ever reaching the upper one. As a result, the minor 3rd, sharp 4th, and minor 7th are sometimes played in a way that emphasizes a pitch somewhere "in the cracks" between equal-tempered pitches. Such pitches are called *blue notes*. Folks who are knowledgeable about microtonal tunings have speculated that these blue notes are actually approximations of the ratios 7:4 (for the minor 7th), 7:5 (for the sharp 4th), and 7:6 (for the minor 3rd). For practical purposes, I think it's easier to consider that the intent of blue notes is to escape the confines of the 12-note equal-tempered scale. When any note within the scale starts sounding a little bit predictable and "safe," leaving the scale entirely is a way of adding emotional meaning to the music.

One final note, before we leave the subject of scales: The blues scale tends to be somewhat directional. The melodic phrases in Figures 7-40, 7-42, and 7-43 all end on the lower tonic note. I haven't done a musicological analysis of blues recordings to determine the frequency with which this directionality is exhibited, but it "feels right" to me. As you experiment with the scales in this chapter you might want to keep an eye on how other musicians use them to form melodic phrases.

## QUIZ

1. List the Greek modes, and indicate which note is the tonic of each mode if only the white keys on the keyboard are used to play them.
2. Which Greek mode has a raised 4th step? Which modes have a lowered 2nd step?
3. If a melody contains a non-chord tone that is sustained through a chord change so that the note becomes a chord tone in the new chord, what is the non-chord tone called?
4. If a melody moves from one chord tone to another chord tone by means of a non-chord tone between the two chord tones, what is the non-chord tone called?
5. What is the pattern of whole-steps and half-steps in the ascending melodic minor scale?
6. Which minor scale contains an augmented 2nd interval?
7. What Greek mode would you use for soloing over an Fm7 chord? Your answer should be a mode whose tonic note is F.
8. How many whole-tone scales are there? How many diminished scales?
9. How many different tones are there in a pentatonic scale?
10. What is a "blue note"?
11. Which pentatonic scale would you use for soloing over a blues progression in D?
12. What note or notes most often follow the sharp 4th (flat 5th) in a blues scale when the scale is used to play a melody?

# 8

# MORE ABOUT CHORD PROGRESSIONS

Unlike triads and 7th chords, all of which can be listed and explained, the number of possible chord progressions is infinite. Even the number of four-measure progressions in 4/4 in which the chords change only at a quarter-note rate is so large it makes my head hurt. As you write your own music or play music written by others, you'll constantly encounter fresh variations. That's what makes chords and harmony so useful.

Even so, certain types of progressions have been used over and over by various composers, to the point where they've become part of the common vocabulary of harmonic music. So it would be premature to end this book without taking a quick look at a few of the standard chord patterns you'll encounter again and again in your musical life.

## BLUES PROGRESSIONS

The blues scale was introduced in Chapter Seven. But there's another side to the blues, which is arguably even more basic than the scale: Most blues songs use some variation on a common chord progression. In its classic form, this progression is 12 bars long. Musicians often refer to it as "12-bar blues," or even just "12-bar." This progression is widely used in jazz, rock, and other genres as well as in the blues genre itself.

The most basic form of the 12-bar blues progression is shown in Figure 8-1. It's seldom played in precisely this way, but the underlying structure shown is implicit in almost any blues progression you'll encounter. The progression consists

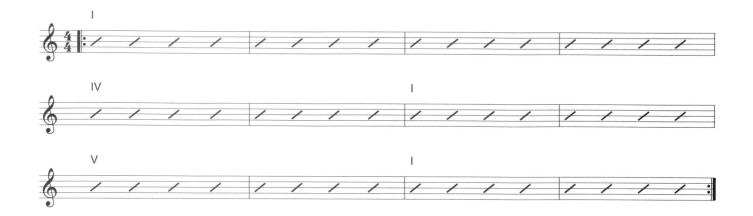

*Figure 8-1. The underlying structure of 12-bar blues uses three four-bar phrases. Most actual blues progressions have one or several added chords not shown here.*

of three four-bar phrases. The first phrase is centered on the I chord. The second phrase starts on the subdominant and returns to the I. The third phrase starts on the dominant, and again there's a return to the I. The entire 12-bar progression is called a chorus. (For more on this term, see below.)

If you take a look back at Figure 4-9, you'll see that it shows an eight-measure progression which is divided into two four-measure phrases. This structure, in which a complete musical idea is built out of two phrases of more or less equal length, is called a *binary form.* Some binary-form phrases are only eight bars long, but others are quite a lot longer. Binary form is hundreds of years old, and is used in everything from Renaissance lute music to punk rock and beyond. One of the things that's interesting about the blues is that the full 12-bar phrase is not binary: The 12-bar blues has a *ternary* (three-part) structure. Blues is the only form of Western music I'm aware of that regularly uses a ternary phrase structure.

Figure 8-1 is a prototype of the blues progression. More typical of blues and blues-derived rock songs is the slightly more complex progression shown in Figure 8-2. In many blues songs, all of the chords in this example would be played as dominant 7ths. There are three differences between this progression and the one in Figure 8-1:

• A IV chord has been added in bar 2.
• Another IV chord follows the V chord in the third phrase, leading back to the I.
• In the last two measures, the chords change more quickly. These measures are called the *turnaround,* because they provide an added impetus that leads forward into the next chorus.

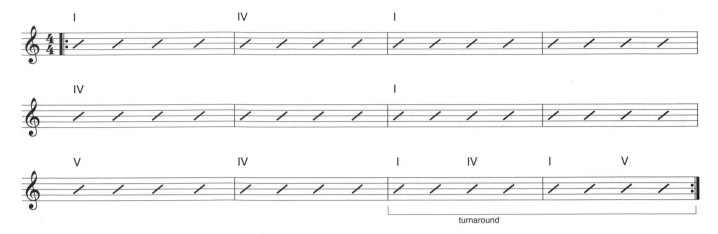

*Figure 8-2. A standard blues progression as it might be played in a jam session. Compared to Figure 8-1, this progression contains an added IV chord in bar 2, another IV in bar 10, and a turnaround in bars 11 and 12. Notice that the harmonic rhythm doubles in the turnaround.*

In jazz, the V and IV chords in bars 9 and 10 are generally replaced with a IIm7-V7 progression. In addition, the turnaround is often played with some type of back-cycling (a progression that moves through a couple of II-Vs or a circle of secondary dominants). A basic jazz blues is shown in Figure 8-3.

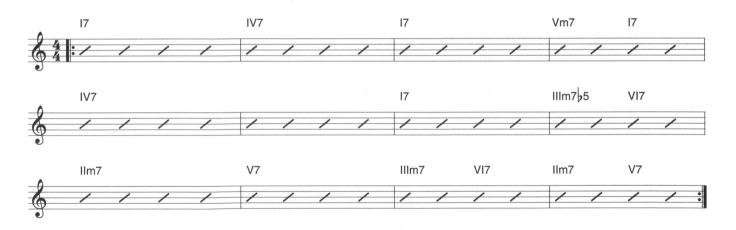

*Figure 8-3. A typical jazz blues progression. In bar 4, the Vm7 and I7 function as a II-V leading up to the IV chord in bar 5. Likewise, the IIm7 chord in bar 9 is preceded by its own secondary II-V. The turnaround (bars 11 and 12) contains two more II-V cycles. Note also that the I chord is not played at the beginning of bar 11. Instead, it's delayed until the beginning of the next chorus.*

Composers often substitute other chords at strategic spots in the blues progression. A ♭VI7, for instance, can substitute for the IV7 in bar 5. The well-known Miles Davis tune "All Blues" (which happens to be in 6/4 rather than 4/4) uses the progression in Figure 8-1, but bar 10 shifts up to a ♭VI chord, falling back to the V in the second half of the bar. In addition, there's some internal movement of voices above the IV root. These extremely simple variations give the tune a distinctive quality that would otherwise be lacking.

Not all blues uses a straight 12-bar framework. In folk blues, whether played on guitar or piano, musicians sometimes add or drop a bar, or even add or drop one or two beats, usually at the end of the four-bar phrase. Stretching and bending the form in this way can give the song a strong emotional impact. Another variant doubles the length of the initial section on the I chord. This is done in many rock and roll songs, so that a four-line verse can be sung over the I. Both the double-length I section and two added beats are used in a Little Richard hit called "Good Golly, Miss Molly." The lyric hook (the title) is sung during an extra two-beat rest that precedes the IV chord.

## VERSE, CHORUS & BRIDGE

The term "chorus" is used by pop and jazz musicians in rather different ways. The term has the same underlying meaning in both genres — the chorus is the memorable part of the song, the part you hope audiences will be humming when they leave the venue after the gig. But the term underwent a sort of transformation in the jazz world.

Jazz as we know it today is an outgrowth of the popular music of the 1920s and 1930s. Many of the popular songs in those bygone days started life as show tunes in Broadway stage musicals. Songs in Broadway shows typically had a verse/chorus structure. Unlike pop music today, though, there was usually only one verse. It was often somewhat introductory in nature, perhaps being sung in a free rhythm over sustained chords. The band or pit orchestra would then enter with a strong beat at the beginning of the chorus. When these tunes were played as instrumentals by jazz bands, the verse, which wasn't very interesting to begin with, was often dropped. Thus, jazz tunes consisting of nothing but a chorus became the norm.

A typical jazz chorus is 32 bars in length, and consists of four eight-bar phrases. The opening eight-bar phrase is played and then repeated, sometimes with small variations. After this 16 bars comes a contrasting eight-bar phrase, called the "middle eight" or "B section." The original eight-bar phrase is then repeated a third time, rounding out the form.

**Diagramming the Form of a Song.** Musicians often give letter-names to the phrases within a song structure, so the structure described above — an eight-bar phrase which is repeated, then a contrasting phrase, and finally the return of the first phrase – is an AABA form. When the form of a song is diagrammed in this way, each letter stands for a separate phrase, and it's reasonable to assume that all of the phrases are the same length (usually four or eight measures). If a section is repeated in a way that's essentially the same as before, but with small variations, the diagram might use subscript numbers to indicate the differences: You might see a song form described as $AA_1BA_2$, for instance, if each repetition of the A section has some variation.

In a piece in which there is no contrasting B section, such as a 12-bar blues or a classical movement in theme-and-variations form, the structure might be diagrammed as $AA_1A_2A_3A_4$. . . . Conversely, a piece in which each section was radically different from what had gone before would have to be diagrammed (if there were any reason to diagram it) as ABCDE. . . .

AABA form is by no means a universal structure for songs that are part of the jazz mainstream. You'll encounter many variants – 32-bar tunes with no middle eight, for instance. (The songbook of the band I'm playing in at the moment includes two beautiful jazz tunes of this type: "All of Me" and "Black Orpheus.") The progressions of such 32-bar tunes may start with an eight-bar phrase, answer it with a different eight-bar phrase, then repeat the first phrase and round out the form with yet a third phrase. This is ABAC form.

When jazz musicians solo over the changes of a standard tune, each soloist will typically take the spotlight for one or several complete choruses, each chorus consisting of the full 32-bar progression. If the performance of the tune is organized in such a way that it begins and ends with a melodic instrument playing the original melody, with improvised solo choruses in between, the musicians may refer to the chorus that contains the original melody as the "head." This is a shortened version of the term "head arrangement," which originally referred to arrangements that were more or less fixed in form, but that weren't written out. They existed only in the musicians' heads.

In pop tunes from the more modern rock tradition, the idea of the verse is still very relevant. Most pop songs today use a structure that alternates verses with choruses. The chord progression used in the verse may or may not be different from the progression used in the chorus. What distinguishes the two is that the lyrics of each verse in the song tend to be different, while the lyrics of all of the choruses in the song tend to be the same. If such a song has three verses, each followed by a chorus, it's in ABABAB form.

In order to provide a little variety, pop songs very frequently have some sort of break after the second chorus. This might be a short instrumental interlude; it might be a longer section in which instrumental solos are played over the chords of the verse, chorus, or both; or it might be a contrasting section in which further lyrics are sung, usually over a different progression than either the verse progression or the chorus progression. The latter type of section is called a *bridge.* It's also called a B section, but this term is a bit misleading. If we diagram a song that has verses, choruses, and a bridge after the second verse, the form would be ABABCAB, making the bridge the C section. (Nobody calls it that, however.)

In songs of this type, the verse, chorus, and bridge can be of any length. Eight-bar and 16-bar phrases are very common, but you might easily run into a song with 32-bar verses and an eight-bar chorus, or vice-versa.

In addition, many songs contain an *intro,* the opening section that precedes the first verse (or, in a jazz chart, the first chorus). The chord progression of the intro may be different from anything else in the arrangement, or it may be drawn from the verse, chorus, or bridge. The part of the song that comes at the very end, after the last chorus, may be called the *outro,* the *tag,* the *ending,* or the *coda.* ("Coda" is a classical music term. It's the Italian word for "tail.") If the last chorus has some special features that lead to the ending, it may be referred to as the "out chorus."

It's generally left up to the performers to devise a suitable tag for a tune. (On the record, the song is likely to fade out.) Often, though not invariably, a short, interesting portion of the chord progression from somewhere near the end of the chorus is repeated two or three times. This is easy for the musicians to remember, and it serves to alert the audience to the fact that the final cadence is only a few bars away.

## BASIC POP PROGRESSIONS

At the risk of looking like a complete idiot, I need to say a few words about the kinds of progressions you're likely to encounter in pop songs. I'm sure I'll leave out dozens of important progressions, so feel free to email me and remind me of your favorites. If or when this book goes into a second edition, I plan to expand this chapter a bit. Looking at unusual progressions found in specific tunes would be useful as well, but instead let's look at ideas that you'll run into again and again.

To begin with, glance at the progression in Figure 8-4. You might hear this type of riff in a hard rock or heavy metal tune, where the open 5ths would be played by a distorted guitar. Clearly, there's a chord progression here. The roots are C and Bb. But are the chords major or minor? The other instruments may fill in the harmony, or they may not. Based on the musical style, it would be reasonable to interpret this as a C minor chord followed by a Bb major. In other words, the whole progression would be in C Dorian or Aeolian. A progression that moves from C major to Bb minor would be interesting, but it's a lot less likely in a hard rock style.

Hard rock tends to favor minor keys. Even when the tonic is major, you'll hear other chords drawn from the diatonic minor scale (bVI, bIII, etc.). The progression

*Figure 8-4. In hard rock, a progression such as this riff may be ambiguous with respect to the major or minor quality of the chords.*

*Figure 8-5. Rock progressions sometimes use chords drawn from the diatonic natural minor. Unlike the V-I root movement typical of jazz, this progression includes two IV-I root movements (from A♭ to E♭, and again from E♭ to B♭).*

in Figure 8-5 might be considered prototypical. Although three of the chords are major, the riff is clearly in C minor.

Progressions in the rock tradition, especially those that are aiming for a serious sound, often avoid or downplay the dominant. Possibly the dominant is felt to be too square or happy-sounding. Try replacing the B♭ chord at the end of Figure 8-5 with a G major chord and you'll hear what I mean. This same trend can be heard in more modern rock styles. The riff in Figure 8-6, which is my own creation, not borrowed from any song in particular, uses the diatonic III chord in place of the V chord one might expect at this point in the riff. If you try replacing the III (A minor) with a V (C) you'll hear how much less satisfying the latter chord would be. After repeating this riff for a total of six bars, I rounded out the eight-bar progression with a V chord — but here again, moving from the V directly back to the I would be unbearably square. A deceptive cadence in which the V is followed by a minor II is more satisfying.

At the other extreme, much of the pop music in the Mexican tradition relies heavily on tonic-dominant progressions. The simplified example in Figure 8-7 may be as offensively inauthentic to Mexican musicians as Figure 8-6 is to grunge rockers, but it illustrates the idea. Some tunes use this I-V-V-I progression throughout, relying on changes in the melody to provide structure and contrast.

Various genres develop their own preferred progressions. Reggae, for example, relies heavily on I-IV riffs, with an occasional V thrown in. Country music is dependent on I, IV, and V as well, due primarily to its origins in bluegrass. More modern country songs sometimes borrow from pop and rock to the extent of

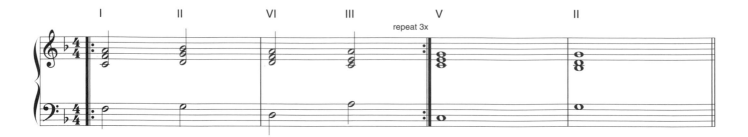

Figure 8-6. A more modern rock progression, which avoids the V-I relationship. The III-I progression at the repeat feels fresher.

Figure 8-7. Some forms of ethnic music rely heavily on V-I progressions. This riff, which makes extensive use of parallel 3rds in the melody, is vaguely Mexican.

Figure 8-8. A progression can be outlined simply by moving the bass while keeping the other notes almost static.

Figure 8-9. You've heard this generic pop ballad progression on the radio. It has been used in hundreds of tunes.

*Figure 8-10. To do something fresh with the progression in Figure 8-9, you might try something like this.*

throwing in the odd diatonic minor (II, III, or VI), but more adventurous progressions are still fairly rare in country, presumably because the intended audience would reject them as too sophisticated or "slick."

Individual arrangers find their own ways of imparting a personal stamp to standard progressions. No discussion of pop chord riffs would be complete (not that the present discussion aims at completeness — anything but) without a sidelong glance at Randy Newman's ability to outline a chord progression by moving nothing but the bass note, while the right-hand piano part remains almost completely static. The riff in Figure 8-8, which is similar to the riff in Newman's hit "Short People," illustrates the idea. The progression, which is basically I-VI-IV-V, is ancient, but this treatment gives it considerable power.

The progression in Figure 8-9 has been used in so many pop ballads that it has acquired generic status. It's not hard to see why: The descending bass line, which you've already met in Figure 7-8, is very natural, and pretty much defines the progression. If you're planning to use this progression in one of your own songs, you may want to consider spicing it up somehow. I've attempted this in Figure 8-10. The chromatic bass movement and altered chords I chose may or may not suit you; the point of this illustration is to suggest that there are ways to work with familiar progressions to make them fresh.

## MODULATION

The chord progressions shown so far in this book all have one thing in common: They're in the same key from beginning to end. While the same observation could be made about much of the music written using chords, it's by no means a universal rule. Many pieces change key during the course of the piece. Some pieces start in one key and end in another; others start and end in the same key, but wander off into a different key for a while in the middle. Sometimes the key change is indicated by a change in key signature in the written score, but if the key change is temporary, the composer may elect to keep the existing key signature and simply add accidentals where necessary.

The general term used for key changes is *modulation.* (Sorry, synthesizer players: This isn't something you can do with your mod wheel.) When the perceived tonal center of the music — the note that's felt to be the tonic — changes, we say the music has modulated to a new key.

Modulation has been widely practiced since the earliest days of tonal music. In music of the Baroque and early Classical periods, most modulations were to closely related keys — from a major key to its relative minor, for example. More than any other composer, it was Beethoven who threw open the floodgates of modulation. Even in his early works he had few compunctions about modulating to almost any key at almost any time. Beethoven always had a strong sense of the original key of the piece he was writing, however. He used remote keys to introduce emotional contrasts.

In the Baroque and early Classical tradition, modulation from the tonic to the dominant and back again was a primary structural or organizational element. This type of modulation was used in thousands of pieces, and until you learn how to listen for it you'll be missing one of the most fundamental aspects of the music. Bach, for instance, wrote hundreds of two-part pieces in which the first part modulated to the dominant and the second part modulated back to the tonic. The main variant in his modulation formula was that a piece in a minor key might modulate either to the dominant or to the relative major.

In the late 18th century, this relatively simple structure of tonic-to-dominant-to-tonic modulation evolved into *sonata form.* (If you'd like to know just about everything there is to know about sonata form, I can recommend Charles Rosen's masterful book *Sonata Forms*, which is published by Norton.) Briefly, a movement in sonata form usually has two main themes. At the beginning of the movement, the first theme is played in the key of the tonic. After a modulation, the second theme is played in the key of the dominant. At the end of the movement, the two themes are stated again — but this time, there's no modulation: The second theme stays in the key of the tonic.

The underlying emotional trajectory of such a piece is fairly clear: The music starts at a particular point (consider it "home"), travels to some other spot, and then returns home. A given movement is, on a psychological level, the equivalent of a journey. While the external forms used in today's popular music are entirely different from sonata form, the underlying emotional trajectory is exactly the same. The middle eight in an AABA jazz chorus or the bridge in a pop song is somewhat removed from the starting point — quite often by being in a different key, or at any rate using a different chord progression. The final A phrase or the final verse and chorus provides a return to the starting point, and rounds out the piece with a feeling of completion.

If you're curious how classical composers used modulation, there's no better way to learn than to study a few scores while listening to the CDs. Modulation is perhaps less important for pop musicians, but that doesn't mean it's a topic we can afford to ignore.

The simplest way to modulate is just to jump straight into the new key. This type of modulation is shown in Figure 8-11. How well it works in a given case will depend on the musical context. You'll note that the phrase in C major in this figure is an authentic cadence. Since a new phrase is about to begin in any case, listeners can more easily perceive the new tonal center without confusion if the previous phrase ends unambiguously. The fact that I've modulated from C major to E major, a relatively distant key, is also significant. This type of abrupt modulation wouldn't work nearly as well if the new key were F major or G major, because the ear would interpret the opening tonic chord of the new phrase as a subdominant or dominant in the key of C. The E major triad is not diatonic in the key of C, so it serves as an immediate signal that something new is happening harmonically, even before the V and IV chords confirm that E is a new tonic.

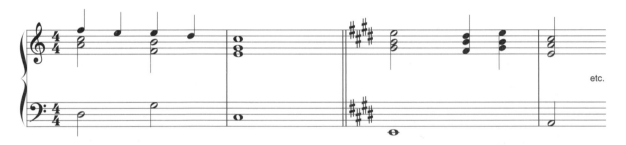

Figure 8-11. The simplest way to modulate: Finish a phrase in one key and then start the next phrase in the new key.

To make modulations less ambiguous, composers often prepare the modulation by preceding the tonic chord of the new key with its own dominant 7th, or even with a IIm7-V7. The modulation in Figure 8-12, for instance, is pretty much a cliché, but it's sometimes the right tool for the job, at least if you're writing in the mainstream ballad style popularized in the 1980s by Barry Manilow. The II-V modulations shown in Figures 8-13 and 8-14 are somewhat less hackneyed, and sound very natural: The ear is easily led to perceive the new key.

If you study modulation in the tradition of 19th-century classical music, you'll soon encounter the term *pivot chord*. A pivot chord is a chord that belongs to both the old key and the new one. A progression starts out in one key, hits the pivot chord, and pivots into the new key. The pivot chord is a sort of musical pun: It has two distinct meanings, depending on whether you're looking backward

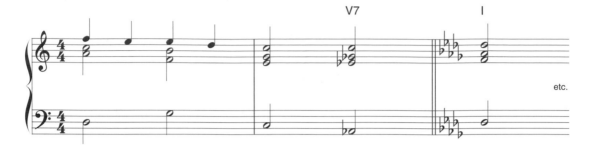

*Figure 8-12. Modulating up by a half-step is easy. Note that the tonic in the old key (C) becomes the leading tone in the new key. This gives the half-step modulation a lift. You can modulate to any key, however, by starting with a dominant 7th in the new key.*

*Figure 8-13. Introducing a new key with a IIm7-V7 progression.*

(at the old key) or forward (at the new one). The progression in Figure 8-15 uses a pivot chord (A minor) to modulate from the key of C major to the key of G major. This chord is found in both keys: It's the diatonic VI triad in C and the diatonic II triad in G.

The success or failure of the pivot-chord modulation technique depends on how ready the ear is to accept the new key. The modulation in Figure 8-15, for instance, wouldn't work well if the ear interpreted the G major triad in the second measure as a V chord in C. This is a particular difficulty when the two keys have such a close relationship. Classical composers sometimes went to considerable lengths to lead the ear astray, so that this particular modulation (upward by a perfect 5th from the tonic to the dominant) would sound natural. In the first movement of Mozart's *Eine Kleine Nachtmusik*, which is in sonata form, the modulation from the first theme in C major to the second theme in G major climaxes with a strong half-cadence on a D chord, the dominant of the new key. When the second theme begins with a resolution of this dominant, the new key is readily accepted by the ear as a tonic. Classical composers weren't always so punctilious about

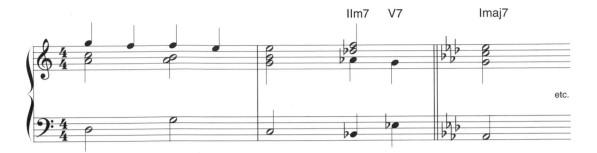

Figure 8-14. The IIm7-V7 progression allows us to modulate to almost any key. The first measure and a half here are the same as in Figure 8-13, but after the Imaj7 in C, we branch off in a different direction.

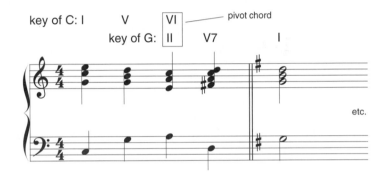

Figure 8-15. Modulation using a pivot chord. The A minor triad here is a VI chord in the key of C, and also a II chord in the key of G.

their modulations, however. Haydn often ended the first theme of a sonata-form movement on a half-cadence in the original key, and then simply launched the second theme on the same chord, which was now the tonic in the new key. This procedure may be less satisfying to modern listeners than it was in Haydn's day.

## DIMINISHED 7TH CHORDS IN PROGRESSIONS

Some chords are even more ambiguous than the pivot chord in Figure 8-15. Take a look at the diminished 7th chord in Figure 8-16, for instance. It's not diatonic in any key, but what if we look at it as the upper voices of a 7♭9 chord? This is the standard interpretation of a diminished 7th in classical harmony theory. This one diminished 7th chord can easily substitute for a dominant 7th in any of four keys: It can function as an F7♭9, a D7♭9, a B7♭9, or an A♭7♭9, depending on which root we play. A classic way to use this ambiguity is to play a diminished 7th chord by itself and then lower one of its tones (any of them — it doesn't matter which) by a

*Figure 8-16. A diminished 7th chord (shown in the treble clef here) is harmonically ambiguous. The same four notes can form a 7♭9 chord with any of four roots.*

*Figure 8-17. Because of the ambiguity shown in Figure 8-16, a diminished 7th chord can resolve in any of four different directions. Dropping any note in the chord by a half-step creates a dominant, which can then move to its own tonic.*

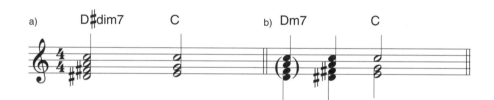

*Figure 8-18. A diminished 7th chord can resolve through chromatic movement of the lower voices (a). One way to look at this progression is that the diminished chord is the result of chromatic movement in the lower voices from a IIm7 chord, as in (b). This chord may not actually be present in the progression, however.*

*Figure 8-19. Instead of resolving a diminished 7th chord, as in Figure 8-17 or 8-18, we can let it slide downward chromatically.*

half-step to create a dominant 7th chord. Figure 8-17 shows how this type of progression works. A diminished 7th chord is thus an effective pivot for modulation to a variety of distant keys.

Another very natural way to resolve a diminished 7th chord is by moving its lowest two voices upward by a half-step to form a major triad in first inversion. This resolution is shown in Figure 8-18a. If you analyze this chord as a D7♭9 with no root, the resolution to C major may not seem very sensible. A better theoretical explanation for why it sounds good is that the D♯ and F♯ are passing tones, as in Figure 8-18b.

Still another way to use diminished 7th chords in a progression is to slide downward chromatically, as in Figure 8-19. This sounds very smooth and natural, because each of the voices is moving by half-steps (for more on voice leading, see below), but there's no way to know how the progression will resolve. We could be modulating to any key at all.

## PEDAL TONES

Instead of branching off to an entirely new key, a progression can remain obsessively anchored in one key, even when you might expect it to move. The device with which this is done is called a *pedal tone*, or simply a pedal. The term comes from pipe organ music: A pipe organ is equipped with a bank of footpedals, which are connected to low-pitched pipes. For the most part, the pedals are used to play slower-moving lines, which makes sense, as our feet are not our most agile appendages. A dramatic effect is achieved in organ writing by jamming a foot down on one note (usually the tonic or dominant) and keeping it there while the hands play a moving passage above the sustained pedal tone. This is often done at the climax of a piece. The idea is illustrated in Figure 8-20.

The ear will accept almost any dissonance as harmonically coherent when it's part of a pedal-tone passage, because the pedal is strong enough to guide the ear toward the expected harmonic resolution. The chromatically moving chords in Figure 8-21 provide an example of this.

*Figure 8-20. A vaguely jazzy progression over a pedal tone.*

*Figure 8-21. Dissonances can work well when an unmoving pedal provides a foundation. The ear tends to interpret the upper notes as passing tones rather than as a free-standing chord progression.*

## VOICE LEADING

For the most part, in this book we've been looking at chords as essentially *vertical* objects — groups of notes that are all played at once. But music is a time-based art. In any piece of music, sonorities follow one another in a *horizontal* manner. When we start connecting chords to one another to form progressions, it's not enough to think about which chord follows or precedes which other chord. The question of how we move from one chord to another becomes important.

In Chapter One, we introduced the idea that a chord is made up of separate voices, each of which sounds exactly one note in the chord. When the progression calls for a new chord, each voice in the first chords must do one of four things: It can play the same note as before (if the two chords contain a suitable *common tone*). It can move upward to a new note. It can drop downward to a new note. Or, if the new chord contains more or fewer voices than the old chord, a voice can stop or start.

The activity of the various voices is called *voice leading*. In the study of voice leading, a chord progression is viewed not as a series of vertical sonorities but as a group of independently moving horizontal lines. We can look, first, at how each voice moves on its own, and second, at how the various voices are moving during transitions from one chord to another. For example, are they all moving upward, or are some moving upward while others move downward?

The earliest music in the Western tradition (written during the Middle Ages) was choral music, and the vertical sonorities employed (chords, in other words) were all a result of the movement of actual voices. Music theorists in those days developed some fairly elaborate rules about voice leading — rules that are, though not entirely irrelevant today, of marginal value in pop music arrangements. Most books on classical harmony theory provide extensive information on voice leading as it was practiced by Bach and other composers in the ensuing 150 years.

In such books, you'll encounter some specific rules. Parallel 5ths, for instance — the simultaneous movement of two voices from one 5th interval to another, as in Figure 8-4 — are explicitly forbidden. At least, they're forbidden for students. Composers from this period did occasionally use parallel 5ths, though they usually avoided them. Theorists, however, sometimes try to explain away the parallel 5ths, or make excuses for them. In Piston's *Harmony*, for instance, it's asserted that a passage in Beethoven's *Symphony No. 6* that contains parallel 5ths "can probably be attributed to inadvertence." In other words, Beethoven didn't notice the parallel 5ths; if he'd noticed them, he'd have fixed the "mistake." The tendency to prefer theoretical correctness to actual scores written by actual composers is perhaps more common in the academic world than it ought to be. I'm more inclined to give Beethoven the benefit of the doubt. I suspect he used the parallel 5ths on purpose, because that was the sound he wanted at that particular spot. In case you're curious, I've reproduced the passage in question in Figure 8-22.

Academic fussing aside, it's probably worthwhile to know the "rules" for classical voice leading. For one thing, knowing them will help you appreciate the vast body of music written by European composers in the 18th and 19th centuries, most of which relies on these rules in almost every measure. In addition, once you know the rules you can violate them intentionally when you want to do so, rather than stumbling into awkward voice leading by accident. Parallel unisons, octaves, and 5ths were avoided because they sounded too strong. They gave an undue weight to the movement from one chord to the next, while tending to obscure the separate movement of the individual voices.

*Figure 8-22. If you take music theory in college, you won't be allowed to use parallel 5ths, but Beethoven did it in this well-known passage, which appears near the beginning of the first movement of his Symphony No. 6. Between bars 3 and 4, the top voice moves downward from C to G while the bottom voice moves down from F to C.*

The movement of voices by augmented and diminished intervals was also avoided. This was because the principles of voice leading were developed at a time when actual voices (human singers) were being employed, and augmented and diminished intervals are difficult to sing. Here again, this "rule" was occasionally violated, for good reason and with good effect, by composers of the period (see Figure 8-23).

*Figure 8-23. Using augmented or diminished intervals in the movement of a voice is often considered a bad idea — but Mozart got away with it in the first movement of his Symphony No. 40.*

One important question to ask about the voice leading in a passage is whether the voices move smoothly (that is, using small intervals), or whether there are a lot of large leaps. The technical term for motion that includes leaps of a 4th or more is *disjunct* motion. Some theorists consider any movement other than by step to be disjunct. Figure 8-24 may give you an idea of how the choice of smooth or disjunct voice leading can affect the sound of a progression. The two examples in this figure use the same progression (ignoring a couple of inversions). In the first example, the largest interval used by any voice in moving from chord to chord is a 3rd. In the second example, larger leaps, including some of more than an octave, are used.

Please note: I'm not saying the first example is better than the second one. The first one has a fairly dull, conventional sound, in fact, while the second one is arguably more interesting. All I'm saying is that when moving from chord to chord, it's important to think about whether you're using smooth or disjunct motion. If you use a series of chords that are connected with smooth voice leading and then suddenly switch to disjunct voice leading (or vice-versa), you'll be creating a contrast that may add a lot of interest to the passage.

The two most important voices in a progression are the top and bottom voices. This is because they're the easiest for the ear to pick out. If you're playing a chording instrument, other instruments may be playing the actual melody and bass line, but for purposes of looking at the chord part itself, we can talk about the top voice as the melody and the bottom voice as the bass line.

When two voices both move up or down at the same time, and both move by the same interval, we say that they're moving in *parallel motion*, as in the example of parallel 5ths given above. If they both move in the same direction but move

Figure 8-24. A two-bar progression, voiced first with smooth voice leading and then with radically disjunct voice leading.

by different intervals, they're engaging in *similar motion.* If one voice moves up while the other moves down, they're moving in *contrary motion.* Parallel and similar motion between the melody and bass line tends to give the chord part a solid, somewhat rigid quality, as Figure 8-25 shows. It's especially noticeable when the melody and bass line move by the same interval.

If all of the voices of the chords move up or down by the same interval, as in the first measure of Figure 8-25, essentially the entire chord is moving up or down as a block. This is occasionally a good strategy when you want to make an emphatic statement, but connecting more than two or three chords in a row by means of rigid parallel motion will give your music a dull, stiff character. It shows a lack of imagination. Introducing some contrary motion where appropriate will give the music a more supple sense of movement. Contrary motion between the top and bottom voices tends to sound good, because it emphasizes their identities as independent lines.

When a voice moves by leap rather than by step, it's usual for the note following the leap to fall back toward the starting point, as shown in Figure 8-26. The larger the leap, the more desirable it is for the melody to move back in the other

Figure 8-25. In bar 1, all of the voices move in parallel motion: The chord moves as a block. In bar 2, there is some contrary motion in the inner voices, but the bass line and melody continue to move in parallel. Between bars 1 and 2, the top and bottom voices move in similar motion (the same direction, but by different intervals).

Figure 8-26. When a voice uses disjunct motion, it's normal for the next note following the leap to fall back toward the starting point.

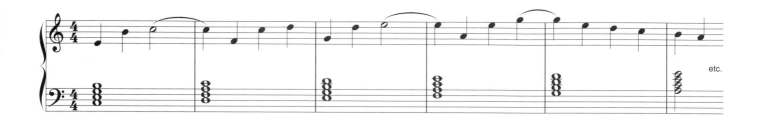

Figure 8-27. While the treatment of disjunct motion shown in Figure 8-26 is the norm, violating the norm is not unheard of. This original melody, which begins with the same notes as "Bewitched, Bothered, and Bewildered," shows another way of treating leaps. As in the melody of "Bewitched," the repeated violation of the norm creates a sort of gravitational pull, which more or less demands that the final leap be followed by a more extended fall (in this case, the E-D-C-B-A at the end) back toward the starting point.

direction as a stabilizing force. Here again, however, the "rule" is anything but absolute. The original melody in Figure 8-27, in which upward leaps of a 5th are followed by another upward-moving interval, sounds perfectly natural.

Another important aspect of voice leading is where you start and where you end up. Generally speaking, moving upward conveys a sense of increasing intensity. This is especially true with respect to melodic movement: The emotional peak of a phrase is often the point at which the highest melody notes are played or sung. If all of the voices of a chord are high, a feeling of great excitement can be generated.

Moving the bass line upward doesn't have quite so clear-cut an effect. This is because the music will sound more full and have a greater impact when the bass part is lower rather than higher. If the melody and bass move in contrary motion, the bass will reach its lowest point as the melody reaches its highest point. This can be a moment of great power. An unusually high bass part can also produce an intense effect, however. You may find it useful to play with this factor in your own arrangements.

Chordal parts seem to sound best when most of the chords use about the same number of voices. To see why, try playing the music in Figure 8-28. The first riff in this figure sounds balanced and logical, not only because of the smooth voice lead-

*Figure 8-28. It's generally a good idea to use about the same number of voices in each chord. The first riff here utilizes three-voice chords in the right hand. The second riff is very similar, except that the right hand switches between five-voice chords and two-voice chords.*

ing (only one of the upper voices moves, and then by half-step) but because the right-hand voicings in the two chords have the same number of voices. By comparison, the second riff sounds more than a bit odd. It's almost as if we're hearing two chording instruments, one of which is being cut out by an intermittent electrical problem. Again, this is not necessarily a bad effect. Moving unexpectedly from a thick chord voicing to a thin one or vice-versa can add real emotional depth. But if you do it routinely and casually, your music will have a disjointed quality that your listeners will have to struggle with.

Because voices outline chords, it's sometimes open to debate whether passing tones in one or two voices should be analyzed as producing an entirely new chord, or whether momentary harmonies produced by passing tones should be ignored in an analysis of the progression. Figure 8-29 provides an illustration of this. The underlying progression in measure 1 is clearly from a Dm7 to a G7♭13. The two chords in the middle of the measure are produced by the motion of what classical theorists would call the soprano and tenor voices. The fact that there's no root movement between the two D chords, and again none between the two G chords, lends weight to the idea that the two chords in the middle of the measure aren't quite real. The voice leading through passing tones in Figure 8-30 is similar, but here I would tend to analyze each chord as being an independent part of the progression, because the roots are moving.

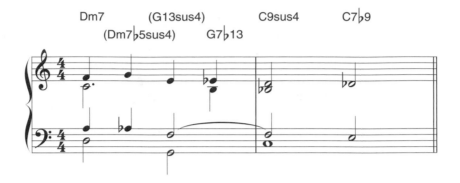

*Figure 8-29. The movement of individual voices sometimes creates temporary harmonies. The basic chord progression in measure 1 here is between the Dm7 and the G7♭13; the two chords in the middle of the measure are less significant. Note that as a chromatic passing tone, the A♭ is moving toward G. Because this is a four-voice texture, however, doubling the root of the G chord wouldn't leave enough voices to provide harmonic color. The G in the upper voice is an incomplete neighboring tone — that is, the underlying movement of this voice is from F to G and back to F. If the second F were played, the G would be an ordinary (complete) neighboring tone. The parallel major 7th adds interest to the voice leading.*

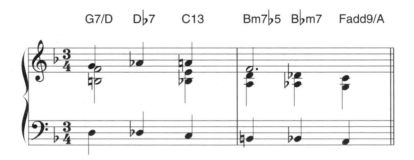

*Figure 8-30. As in Figure 8-29, passing harmonies are created in this progression by smooth movement of the voices. The underlying progression is G7-C13-Fadd9. Because the passing chords have their own roots, however, they'll be more readily heard as independent parts of the progression. Note that the A♭ in measure 1 and the B♮ in measure 2 violate the principles of enharmonic spelling discussed in Chapter Seven. The spellings shown are preferable, however, because they make the chords easier to read.*

## GERMAN & NEAPOLITAN 6THS

If you listen to classical music written between 1780 and 1880, you'll often hear a few non-diatonic chords that add to the palette of chord progressions: the family of augmented 6th chords and the Neapolitan 6th. None of these is a 6th chord in the sense in which jazz musicians use the term; the reasons why they're called 6th chords will become clear as we proceed.

The German 6th is the enharmonic equivalent of a dominant 7th chord built on the flatted 6th step of the scale — ♭VI7. We've already seen this type of chord a couple of times in this book. In Figure 8-12, for instance, it provides a pivot in a modulation. However, the German 6th is not called a 6th chord because it's built on the 6th step of the scale. (Nor is there anything German about it.) It gets its name from the enharmonic spelling of the 7th of the chord as an augmented 6th. Figure 8-31 shows this spelling (an A♭7 chord in C major in which the 7th of the chord is spelled as F♯ rather than G♭), and also shows a characteristic use of the chord.

*Figure 8-31. The German 6th chord (the second chord in measure 1) gets its name from the augmented 6th interval between its root and the upper note. In classical music, it most often precedes either a I chord in second inversion, as shown here, or a V chord.*

Note the smooth chromatic voice leading with which the A in the F chord proceeds downward to the G in the bass of the second-inversion C chord, while the F moves upward to the top G. When using this progression, a classical composer would probably have spelled the E♭ enharmonically as a D♯, because that voice resolves upward to the E. Spelled with a D♯, the chord is sometimes referred to as an English 6th. (Again, there's nothing especially English about it.) If the D♯/E♭ is replaced with a D♮, the chord is called a French 6th. The French 6th in C is enharmonically the same as a D7♭5 or A♭7♭5 chord.

The Neapolitan 6th is a major triad built on the flatted 2nd step of the scale — for example, a D♭ triad in the key of C. It gets its name from the fact that it was originally heard most often in first inversion, which meant there would be an interval of a 6th between the bass note and the root of the chord. During the common practice period, the Neapolitan was used most often when the music was in a minor key, as in the progression in Figure 8-32.

Note that the secondary dominant of the Neapolitan (V7 of ♭II) is enharmonically the same as the German 6th. Composers like Mozart and Haydn routinely used this fact to modulate temporarily to the key of the ♭II, in the manner shown in Figure 8-33. After arriving at the ♭II chord, they might stay in this key for several bars before returning to the original key.

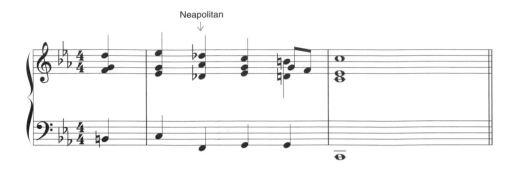

Figure 8-32. The Neapolitan 6th chord (which is not a 6th chord) is a major chord built on the flatted 2nd step of the scale. As this passage shows, in classical music it was most often used in a minor key, and functioned more or less as a substitution for the II chord, which in the natural minor scale would be a diminished triad.

Figure 8-33. The German 6th (a ♭VI7 chord) can be used as a secondary dominant leading to the Neapolitan chord (A♭7 to D♭ in the key of C).

## HOW TO COMP FROM A CHORD CHART

Theoretical knowledge is a wonderful thing, no doubt, but the point of learning about chords is to be able to use them in actual musical situations. Unless you're strictly a classical musician or composing your own material, that probably means playing from chord charts.

There's a lot more to playing from a chart than understanding what notes are used in the chords on the chart. First and foremost, you need a thorough working knowledge of your instrument. But even if you're a virtuoso, your ability to comp (accompany) will depend on your familiarity with the musical style you're being called on to play. Country, pop, Latin, jazz, and blues all have their own characteristic rhythms and chord voicings, and a player who is proficient in one style may be a complete duffer in another.

Sadly, I don't have the kind of encyclopedic knowledge of styles that would allow me to give you the Seven Basic Country Strums, 20 Ultimate Jazz Licks, or whatever. I can, however, suggest some guidelines that will help you sharpen your skills.

**Learn the style you want to play.** Buy CDs and listen to them analytically. Focus on what *your* instrument is doing in each song. Listen to the rhythms and the chord voicings. Notice how the parts played by your instrument fit with those played by other instruments. Analyze the chord progressions. Go to concerts and listen to the same things.

**Practice with a metronome.** Comping is all about getting from one end of the tune to the other with no serious mistakes. Staying with the rhythm is essential. In the heat of a concert, it's often preferable to play a wrong note rather than fumble around and lose the groove. If you're having trouble with a particular chord, slow the metronome down and practice the entire song until you can move through the troublesome chord without hesitation.

**Listen to the other players.** Listen to their rhythms and chord voicings. If two instruments are chording in the same range, the sound will tend to be cluttered, so you may need to move your voicings up or down to a pitch range that isn't so busy. You may also discover that you're playing a minor 9th (which is called for in the chart) while someone else is steadfastly playing a natural 9th. Depending on the situation, you might choose to change what you're playing or to point out the problem to the other player in a tactful way.

Rhythm playing seems to work best when the various instruments accent some of the same beats, but not all of them. If there are anticipations in a chord chart (places where the new chord starts half a beat ahead of the bar line) it's especially important for the whole band to be together. Throwing an accent into a hole — a spot where the other players are resting — can add a lot of interest to your part. As long as it's the right accent, of course.

**Memorize the charts.** Chord progressions have their own logic and flow, which generally makes them pretty easy to memorize. Many charts, however, contain one or two tricky spots where your ear may lead you astray. If necessary, use verbal reinforcement: At the beginning of the tune, remind yourself, "First time A minor, second time A7," or whatever.

**Analyze the charts.** Chords don't exist in a vacuum. In a well-written piece of music, each chord leads to the next one in a logical way. You might discover, for instance, that all of the chords in the bridge are drawn from a D major scale. The fact that they have lots of common tones might suggest certain types of voicings that wouldn't occur to you if you were just looking at a series of roots.

## THE OUT CHORUS

In this book I've tried to set out the basic tools musicians need for understanding chords and harmony. Given the vastness of the subject matter, to say nothing of my own slightly less than encyclopedic knowledge and my publisher's very reasonable assessment that you probably wouldn't want to buy a 700-page book, the treatment has inevitably been sketchy at times. To become a master of the harmonic universe, you'll need to explore further on your own. The tools you'll need — scores, recordings, performances by your favorite musicians, and your own instrument(s) of choice — are readily accessible. The harmonic vocabulary available to musicians in the 21st century is not only vast but capable of amazing subtleties of expression. Knowing the vocabulary is essential for any serious musician, but what you choose to say with it is entirely up to you.

Happy harmonizing!

## QUIZ:

1. What is it called when the harmonic rhythm doubles in the last two bars of a blues progression?
2. How many four-bar phrases are there in each chorus of a typical blues song?
3. Define the term "chorus" as it's used in jazz.
4. What is a tag?
5. What term is used to describe a progression in which the music changes to a new key?
6. What is an unchanging bass note called?
7. What term is used to describe the chord voicing technique in which one voice moves upward while another moves downward?
8. What is the root of a Neapolitan 6th chord in the key of D major? What note would usually appear in the bass?

# APPENDIX A:
## HOW TO READ SHEET MUSIC

First and foremost, music is about making sounds. The question of how to write down a set of instructions that will enable others (or enable you yourself at a later date) to recreate the sounds is only of secondary importance. On the other hand, no matter how fantastic you are at playing your instrument, if you don't know how to read music notation you're going to be at a serious disadvantage when it comes to communicating your ideas to other musicians, and at understanding their communications in return.

The purpose of this Appendix is not to provide an exhaustive treatment of the minutiae of music notation. The goal is much simpler: to enable you to understand and interpret the printed examples in this book. Many details (such as ties, triplets, and articulation marks) are omitted entirely. If you're interested in learning more, the standard reference work to dive into is *Music Notation*, by Gardner Read [Taplinger].

I'm going to assume you have access to a keyboard instrument of some kind. A piano is ideal, but electronic keyboards have at least one advantage: They never go out of tune. Learning to read music starting with an instrument other than a piano is eminently feasible, but few other instruments let you play chords with as much freedom, or provide as much visual feedback on the shape of the chord while you're doing it. Since being able to find, play, and understand chords is the point of this book, we're going to use the keyboard as the basis for explaining notation. Whether you ever acquire any keyboard dexterity or simply pick out the examples one note at a time is entirely up to you.

**The Staff.** Most music is written on a five-line horizontal template called a *staff* (plural *staves*). Each line and each space on the staff corresponds to one of the white keys on the keyboard. Each of the keys sounds a specific musical pitch, and each of the pitches has a letter-name. The white keys on the keyboard have the letter-names A through G; these letters are repeated up and down the keyboard, as shown in Figure A-1.

Since there are 52 white keys on an 88-note piano keyboard, and only five lines on the staff (plus the four spaces between the lines), at any given point in the music only a small number of musical pitches can be indicated on any given staff. The symbol that tells us which set of pitches the staff is assigned to is called a *clef.* The clef appears at the left end of each staff. Several clefs are in common use, but

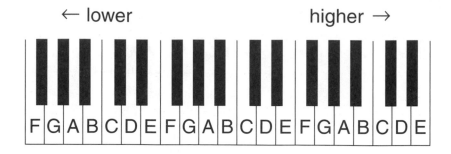

Figure A-1. The white keys on the keyboard have letter-names. Seven letters are used, so the letter-names repeat. Pay close attention to the positions of the black keys in relation to the letter-names. Lower pitches are to the left, higher pitches to the right.

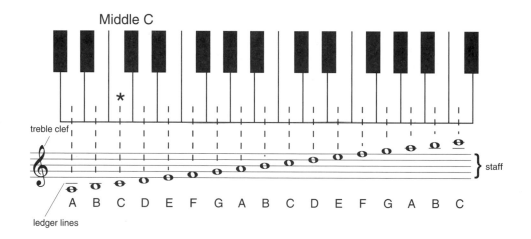

Figure A-2. The treble clef (top) and bass clef (bottom) indicate specific ranges on the keyboard. To find Middle C, locate the lowest C on the keyboard and count upward. If you're using a five-octave electronic keyboard, Middle C is the third C counting up from the bottom. If you're using a piano or equivalent 88-note keyboard, Middle C is the fourth C.

the main ones you need to know about — the only ones used in this book — are the *treble clef* and the *bass clef*. These clefs are shown in Figure A-2.

Mnemonics are often used to remember the letter-names on the staves. In the treble clef, the five lines (from bottom to top) are E, G, B, D, and F, which could stand for "every good boy does fine." The spaces in the treble clef (again, from bottom to top) are F, A, C, and E, which spells "face." In the bass clef, the lines are G, B, D, F, A ("good boys do fine always"), and the spaces are A, C, E, G ("all cows eat grass").

In music written for the piano, two staves are normally employed, as shown in Figure A-3. Together they're known as the Grand Staff.

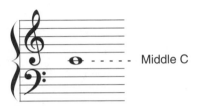

Figure A-3. Piano music is written on the Grand Staff, which combines two staves, one with treble clef and the other with bass clef. Middle C is written with one ledger line either above the bass clef or below the treble clef. In actual sheet music, the treble and bass staves will be further apart; they're placed close together in this figure to make it clear that the ledger line containing Middle C is the only line that would fall between them.

When notes are too high or too low to be placed on a staff, given the clef currently assigned to that staff, short lines are placed above or below the staff so that more lines and spaces are available. These short lines are called *ledger lines*.

**Notes.** To indicate which notes are to be played, dots are placed on the staff. The dots can be either hollow or filled in, and can have stems attached to them or, in some cases, no stem. Actually, noteheads are bigger than dots; dots are also used in notation, and have a different meaning. The vertical position of the notehead on the staff — the line or space where it's placed — indicates which pitch is to be played. The noteheads and the stems attached to them are of various types. Each type indicates a rhythmic *duration*. The duration of a note is the length of time it sustains, from start to finish.

Musicians measure time in *beats*. The beat is a steady pulse, which could come from a metronome or drum machine, from tapping your foot, or from a conductor waving a stick. The pulse may be very slow, or it may be very fast. While the speed of the beats may make a big difference for both the audience and the musicians themselves, it doesn't affect the way the music is notated. A beat will look just the same on paper, whether the speed of the beat (which musicians refer to as the *tempo*) is slow or fast.

A long note may last for a number of beats, while a short note may last for only a fraction of a beat. If 16 notes are crowded into one beat, the music may sound fast to the listeners, even though the beat is slow.

Beats are grouped into *measures*. The most common type of grouping puts four beats into each measure. Other groupings with two, three, five, six, or more beats per measure are also found, but the nomenclature (the naming system) most often used for describing note durations is based on the idea that there are four beats per measure. Measures are separated from one another using vertical lines called *bar lines*.

The type of note that lasts for one beat is called a *quarter-note*. (There are some exceptions to this rule, but we're not going to worry about them in this extremely basic overview.) Quarter-notes and bar lines are shown in Figure A-4. The quarter-note gets its name from the fact that there is room for four of them in a single four-beat measure. A quarter-note has a solid notehead and a vertical stem. The stem can point either up or down. Music engravers have some rules about whether the stem on a particular note should point up or down, but those rules aren't too important when you're first learning to read music.

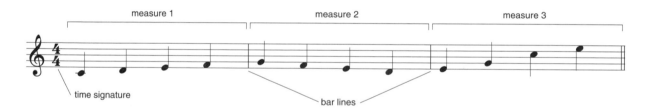

Figure A-4. As explained in Chapter Four, the time signature shows how many beats are included in each measure (the top number) and the type of note that counts for one beat (the bottom number). A time signature appears near the left end of the first staff. In 4/4 time, as shown here, there are four quarter-notes (solid noteheads with stems) in each measure. Measures are separated by bar lines.

Notes that are shorter than quarter-notes have *flags* or *beams* attached to their stems. Notes that are longer than quarter-notes have hollow note-heads. Figure A-5 shows some of the note values that are used most often. When a shorter note appears by itself, it has a flag. When several shorter notes appear together in one beat, the flags are extended horizontally to form one or more beams, which connect all of the notes. The beam shows how the beats are grouped. (Beams are not used for this purpose in vocal music.)

Figure A-5. Each of the types of notes shown has a different length. A quarter-note lasts for one beat; all of the other notes are longer or shorter. There are two quarter-notes in a half-note, two eighth-notes in a quarter-note, four sixteenth-notes in a quarter-note (or two sixteenth-notes in an eighth-note), and so on.

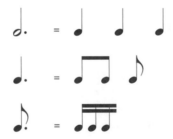

Figure A-6. A dot after a notehead increases its duration by 50%. Since a half-note has the same length as two quarter-notes, a dotted half-note lasts for three quarter-notes, and so on.

Figure A-7. The three half-notes in measure 1 are played together as a chord. Then the two quarter-notes in this measure are played separately, first the E and then the C. In measure 2, the two eighth-notes are played separately, then the three quarter-notes together as a chord, and finally the half-note by itself. While doing this, keep a steady count, as indicated beneath the staff.

The duration of any note can be extended by 50% by placing a dot after the note head, as shown in Figure A-6. For instance, a quarter-note normally has the same length as two eighth-notes, but a dotted quarter-note has the same length as three eighth-notes.

All of the notes that are to be played on the same beat are aligned vertically on the staff. Often, they'll be connected by a single stem. Music is read from left to right, so notes that are positioned horizontally are to be played one after another. While reading the music, it's important to keep a steady beat, so that the lengths of the notes are clear (see Figure A-7).

**Rests.** Since each measure has to have the same total number of beats, special symbols are needed to indicate any beats on which the musician is not supposed to play. These symbols are called *rests*. Figure A-8 shows what rests look like. Rests can be dotted, just like notes.

*Figure A-8. Each note value has a corresponding rest. The rest is the same length as the note. A whole-rest (top) looks a lot like a half-rest (just below it). Here's a mnemonic for remembering which is which: Imagine that the two rests are glued to the lines. The whole-rest needs to have its whole surface covered with glue to keep from falling off, but the half-rest might only be half glued on.*

**Accidentals.** In order to indicate when the black keys on the keyboard are to be played, symbols called *accidentals* are used. The most important three accidentals for you to know about are the flat (♭), the sharp (♯), and the natural (♮). The flat lowers the pitch of a note by a half-step: Instead of playing the white key indicated in Figure A-2, when you see a flat before the note you should play the black key immediately to the left of the white key. If there isn't a black key immediately to the left — if the flat occurs before the note C or F — play the white key immediately to the left instead. The sharp raises the pitch of a note by a half-step, so when you see a sharp before a note you should play the black key immediately to the *right* of the white key (or, if there isn't a black key immediately to the right, as in the case of E and B, play the white key immediately to the right). These options are summarized in Figure A-9. The natural cancels a flat or sharp, so when you see a natural you should play the white key assigned to that line or space, ignoring any flats or sharps that might previously have been applied to that pitch.

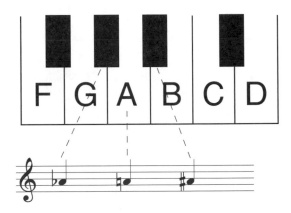

*Figure A-9. The flat before the first quarter-note indicates that the black key below the A should be played. The natural cancels a flat or sharp, indicating that the white key should be played. The sharp before the third quarter-note indicates that the black key above the A should be played.*

Because of the way the keyboard is laid out, each black key can be indicated on the staff in two different ways. It can be written by putting a note on the line or space corresponding to the next lower white key and placing a sharp before the note to raise the pitch. Or the note can be positioned on the line or space corresponding to the next *higher* white key, and a flat can be placed before the note to lower the pitch. Two examples are given in Figure A-10. The rules for whether to call a given black key a flat or a sharp are discussed in Chapter One.

Accidentals are used in two ways. First, an accidental can be placed directly before a single note anywhere on the staff. When this is done, the accidental applies to that note and also to any other note on the same line or space that follows the accidental within the same measure — that is, until the next bar line is reached. A bar line cancels this type of accidental. Second, one or more sharps or flats can be placed at the left end of the staff, immediately after the clef, as shown in Figure A-11. The group of accidentals at the left end of the staff is called the *key signature*. When an accidental appears in the key signature, all of the notes anywhere on the staff that have that letter-name (whether or not they're in the same octave as the accidental) are flatted or sharped.

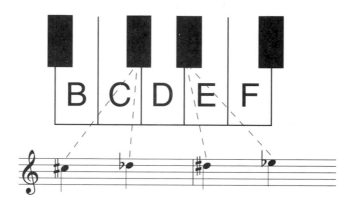

*Figure A-10. A black key can be "spelled" using either of two different letter-names. The black key between C and D can be referred to either as a C♯ or as a D♭, for instance. The black key between D and E, meanwhile, can be referred to either as a D♯ or as an E♭.*

*Figure A-11. The key signature, which appears at the left end of the staff next to the clef, indicates that all notes with the corresponding letter-name are to be played either a half-step higher (if the key signature shows a sharp) or a half-step lower (if the key signature shows a flat) than the white key that would otherwise be played.*

# APPENDIX B:
## THE HARMONIC SERIES & EQUAL TEMPERAMENT

**M**ost music written today, at least in the European/American tradition (which is increasingly dominant around the world), uses a scale consisting of 12 equally spaced pitches. This scale is highly artificial. It was developed in the early 1700s; prior to that time, a number of other tuning systems were in use in European music, and of course in the music of other cultures. In order to explain this scale, we need to take a brief detour to talk, at least briefly, about the *harmonic series.*

Using a process developed by an 18th-century French mathematician named Jean-Baptiste Fourier (pronounced "four-yay"), any sound can be analyzed as the sum of one or more *sine waves,* each of which has its own amplitude, frequency, and phase characteristics. What exactly is a sine wave? The term has a mathematical meaning, but don't worry about it. Think of a sine wave as a sort of sonic atom or building block — the simplest possible sound.

In most tones created by musical instruments (except for drums and a few others), the frequencies of the various sine waves have simple mathematical relationships to one another. All of them are whole-number multiples of the lowest frequency in the tone. In the real world of vibrating physical objects, they may not be exact multiples, but the numbers are close enough that we don't need to worry about any discrepancies.

The lowest frequency is called the *fundamental.* The various sine waves are all called *partials* or *harmonics,* and all of the partials above the fundamental are called *overtones.* So if the fundamental is, for instance, at 110Hz, the tone will contain overtones at 220Hz, 330Hz, 440Hz, and so on, as shown in Figure B-1. Any

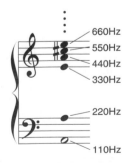

Figure B-1. Most tones in nature consist of numerous partials, which vibrate at frequencies that are whole-number multiples of the lowest partial. The lowest partial is called the fundamental. Shown here is a fundamental frequency of 110Hz (which happens to be an A) and its first five overtones. Note that the overtone series continues upward indefinitely; only the lower overtones are shown.

series of tones that are whole-number multiples of one another is said to be part of the harmonic series, and individual tones within such a series are called harmonics.

If you're interested in a little more academic rigor, you might appreciate knowing the following facts:

**1.** Every sound consists of one or more partials, which are sine waves.

**2.** If the partials are close to being whole-number multiples of some frequency, then this frequency is called the fundamental, and all of the higher partials are called overtones. The second partial (counting from the bottom) is the first overtone.

**3.** If the partials are *not* whole-number multiples of some frequency, the sound is said to be *clangorous* (meaning that it sounds more or less like a bell) or *noisy* (meaning random). In the case of noise, the number of partials is technically infinite, because noise is defined as a signal that contains energy at all frequencies.

Unless the overtones are unusually loud (usually they won't be as loud as the fundamental), our ears will identify the frequency of the fundamental as being the frequency of the tone itself. The other partials, rather than being perceived separately, will contribute to the perceived *tone color* of the tone.

As mentioned in Chapter One, in the section on playing in tune, whenever two tones with different pitches are sounded at once, a third tone called a difference tone can also be perceived. The frequency of the difference tone is the difference (found by subtraction) between the frequencies of the other two tones. Here's the key point: If the partials are harmonically related, as in Figure B-1, the difference tones between partials will *also* be harmonically related. For instance, if two of the partials above a 100Hz fundamental are at 400Hz and 500Hz, then they create a 100Hz difference tone.

In practical terms, what this means is that if you play a low A and an E that's an octave and a 5th above it, the fundamental of the E will be at the same frequency as the second overtone of the A. Your ear will be able to perceive this intuitively: The E and the A will sound pleasant together, because there won't be much (if any) beating between them.

## EQUAL TEMPERAMENT

Looking at Figure B-1, you might assume that our scale is built using the pitches in the natural harmonic series. This assumption would be about half right and half wrong. In fact, the scale used in European/American music is the result of a set of compromises. The intervals in the scale are derived from the harmonic series, but a bit of fudging has been required to make everything come out right.

In order to explain the fudging (and what it means harmonically), we'll have to take a short digression to talk about frequency *ratios*.

A ratio is a relationship between two numbers. We've already noted, in Chapter One, the fact that any note in the scale has twice the frequency of the note an octave below it. Another way to say this is that the frequency ratio between the two notes is 2:1. (If you're reading aloud, you would read this as "two to one.")

A scale comprising no intervals but octaves wouldn't be very interesting. To fill in the octave with other pitches, we need to use other ratios. To build the chromatic scale, our musical ancestors also used the ratios 3:2 and 5:4. These ratios define the intervals of the *perfect 5th* and *major 3rd*. (These intervals are discussed in Chapter Two.)

The discussion that follows may seem a bit abstract. The reason it's important is because the actual sound quality of the chords we use today depends in large part on the relative frequencies of the tones in the chord. This is especially true of major triads.

The 3:2 and 5:4 intervals occur naturally in the real world, because they're part of the harmonic series. In Figure B-1, the distance between the A and C♯ in the treble clef is a ratio of 5:4 (550 divided by 440). No matter what frequency we choose for the fundamental, the frequencies of the fourth and fifth partials will have this ratio, and they'll be a major 3rd apart.

If you have a stringed instrument handy, you can verify this for yourself by playing *harmonics*. A harmonic is played by touching the string lightly while playing it. The string must be touched at a point that divides its length into equal fractions. If you touch the string at the halfway point, for instance, and then play it, you'll hear a tone an octave above the pitch of the open string. For purposes of discussion, let's suppose that the length of the open string is 24 inches. When you touch it at the halfway point, each half vibrates separately, so in effect you're playing two strings, each of which is 12 inches long. Cutting the length in half doubles the frequency. (If you're technically minded, you'll understand that there is an *inverse* relationship between string length and frequency.) The ratio of the string lengths is 24:12, which is the same as 2:1.

When you touch the string at a point exactly 1/3 of the way along its length, it vibrates in three separate segments. The length ratio is 24:8, or 3:1, and the tone produced by the string is an octave and a 5th above the open string. When you touch it at the 1/5 point, it vibrates in five separate segments, producing a 5:1 ratio, which is two octaves and a major 3rd above the open string. Isolating such a high harmonic on a physical string is difficult, but it can be done with bowed instruments.

Without getting into a lot of mathematical detail, we'll merely note that if the string length of the 2:1 (octave) harmonic node is 12 inches, while the string length produced by the 3:1 (octave and a fifth) harmonic node is 8 inches, the ratio of these two string lengths is 12:8, which is the same as 3:2. This is the ratio of the perfect 5th interval.

In the early days, instruments were often tuned so that the pitches of their open strings were in exactly these ratios. But as the black keys were added to the keyboard, and as composers started to use them to produce more complex chords and scales, a vexing difficulty became apparent. Intervals that looked the same size on the keyboard — that encompassed the same number of half-steps — didn't necessarily have the same frequency ratios. Some of them would sound in tune, while others sounded unpleasantly out of tune.

To see why this is the case, let's create a tuning system using nothing but the interval of the perfect 5th. (This is called a Pythagorean tuning, after the semi-mythical Greek mathematician Pythagoras, whose followers first proposed it.) We'll start with a low note, as shown in Figure B-2 and Table B-1, and "stack" per-fect 5ths until we've covered all 12 pitches in the chromatic scale. When we arrive back at B♯, which on the keyboard is the same note as C, we find a discrepancy: The pitch of B♯ is 4,151.88Hz, while the pitch of the C in the same octave is only 4,096Hz. If we play this B♯ and C at the same time, we'll hear rapid beating, be-cause the distance between them is almost 55Hz.

In order to tune B♯ to the same frequency as C, it's necessary to make all of the "perfect" 5ths in the scale just slightly narrower than a perfect 3:2 ratio. If we crunch them together in this manner, we'll end up with a scale in which all of the 5ths are slightly out of tune. This is, in fact, the equal-tempered scale that's used today. It's a compromise, but a fairly effective one. The 5th, which is the basis of much of our music, is very close to 3:2, so it doesn't sound at all bad. If anything, the slow beating gives it a warm character.

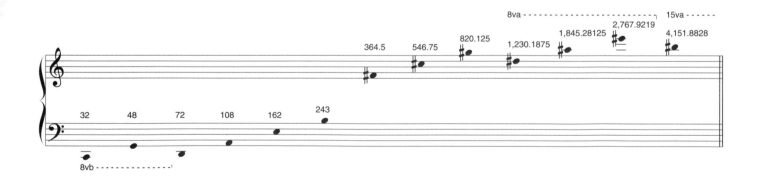

*Figure B-2. Stacking perfect 5ths (which have a 3:2 frequency ratio) is one way to build a 12-note chromatic scale. To make the numbers easier to read, I've given the frequency of C as exactly 32Hz.*

| note | frequency | | note | frequency |
|:---:|:---:|:---:|:---:|:---:|
| C | 32 | | C | 32 |
| G | 48 | | C | 64 |
| D | 72 | | | |
| A | 108 | | C | 128 |
| E | 162 | | | |
| B | 243 | | C | 256 |
| F♯ | 364.5 | | C | 512 |
| C♯ | 546.75 | | | |
| G♯ | 820.125 | | C | 1,024 |
| D♯ | 1,230.1875 | | | |
| A♯ | 1,845.28125 | | C | 2,048 |
| E♯ | 2,767.922... | | | |
| B♯ | 4,151.883... | | C | 4,096 |

*Table B-1. The meaning of Figure 1-7 will be a little clearer if we look at it in this form. In the two left columns, we proceed upward from the lowest C in perfect 5ths (ratio 3:2). Note that I've given C an arbitrary frequency value of 32Hz purely to make the numbers easier to understand. The actual frequency of a low C is not exactly 32Hz. Eventually we arrive at the note B♯. On a keyboard, B♯ is the same note as C. But if we proceed upward in octaves rather than fifths, as shown in the two columns on the right, the frequency of the top C is 4,096Hz, not 4,151.883Hz.*

Here's another way to look at the equal-tempered scale: Each half-step has exactly the same frequency ratio as every other half-step. This allows us to play in any key and have the music sound the same. But in order to divide an octave (a 2:1 ratio) into 12 equal steps, for each half-step we have to use the ratio of the twelfth root of 2 to 1. The 12th root of 2 is an irrational number: It's about 1.059463, but not exactly, since an irrational number by definition has an infinite number of digits following the decimal point. If you multiply 1.059463 by itself 12 times, you'll end up with about 1.999999, which is pretty close to 2.

Remember that we said a major 3rd has a frequency ratio of 5:4. If we tune the note C to 32Hz, for example, as in Table B-2, we would expect that the E above this C would have a frequency of exactly 40Hz (because 40:32 is the same ratio as 5:4). Looking at the equal-tempered scale in Table B-2, however, you may notice something odd: The frequency shown for E is not 40Hz but about 40.317Hz. In other words, the major third in the equal-tempered scale is wider than it would be if it were based on an ideal harmonic ratio.

If we tried to build a chromatic scale using 5:4 major thirds, however, we'd get in trouble immediately. Starting with a 32Hz C and moving upward from C through an augmented triad (C-E-G♯-C), as shown in Figure B-3, we'd arrive at an octave C (actually another variety of B♯) with a frequency of 62.5Hz rather than 64Hz. Thus if we built a scale by stacking 5:4 major thirds, the octave would be noticeably flat. Widening the major 3rd so that stacking three of them gives us a perfect octave produces exactly the same scale as narrowing the perfect 5th so that the B♯ in the Circle of Fifths is the same as C. Either way, we end up with an equal-tempered chromatic scale in which the half-step ratio is the 12th root of 2.

Because the equal-tempered major 3rd is wider than a 5:4 ratio, you'll hear prominent beats when you play this interval. The beats give the equal-tempered major triad a bright, edgy sound. Since you've been hearing this triad all your life, and may even have been taught that it's good-sounding and "consonant" (a term defined in Chapter Two), you may never notice consciously that it isn't actually very restful. My suspicion, however, is that composers in the 19th and 20th

*Figure B-3. Stacking major 3rds that are based on a perfect 5:4 ratio gives us an octave that's noticeably flat. In an equal-tempered scale, the upper B♯ is the same note as C, but here it has a frequency of 62.5Hz rather than the 64Hz that would be an octave above the low C.*

**Circle of Fifths**

| note | frequency |
|------|-----------|
| C | 32 |
| G | 47.946 |
| D | 71.837 |
| A | 107.635 |
| E | 161.269 |
| B | 241.631 |
| F# | 362.037 |
| C# | 542.443 |
| G# | 812.745 |
| D# | 1,217.741 |
| A# | 1,824.549 |
| E# | 2,733.334 |
| B# | 2,048 |

**Chromatic Scale**

| note | frequency |
|------|-----------|
| C | 32 |
| C# / D♭ | 33.903 |
| D | 35.919 |
| D# / E♭ | 38.055 |
| E | 40.317 |
| F | 42.715 |
| F# / G♭ | 45.255 |
| G | 47.946 |
| G# / A♭ | 50.797 |
| A | 53.817 |
| A# / B♭ | 57.017 |
| B | 60.408 |
| C | 64 |

*Table B-2. The frequencies in a Circle of Fifths (left) and a chromatic scale (right) based on the 12th root of 2. Because this is an irrational number, all values shown except those for C are approximate — and as in Table B-1, C is given an arbitrary value of 32Hz.*

centuries went further and further afield harmonically, exploring more and more exotic chord voicings and chord progressions, in no small part because the equal-tempered major triad doesn't sound very good. It doesn't produce a feeling of stability or repose, so composers found themselves avoiding or obscuring it.

Interpreting history, especially the history of art, is a chancy business at best. This theory is highly speculative. A more conservative interpretation would be that the restless energy of the 18th and 19th centuries drove composers to develop new forms of harmonic expression, and that the equal-tempered scale was developed precisely in order to allow them this degree of harmonic freedom. In a more stable culture, the equal-tempered scale might never have arisen, because composers wouldn't have needed it.

In any case, because this book talks about how simple chord voicings can be developed into more complex voicings (as happened during this period in history), it would be irresponsible not to put the development of that harmonic language in some sort of context. Since most musicians never have any reason to venture outside the bounds of the 12-note equal-tempered scale, however, there's no particular reason to say any more about it here.

# APPENDIX C:
## ANSWERS TO THE QUIZZES

## CHAPTER 1:

1. Pitch, rhythm, loudness, and tone color.
2. E major, B♭ major.
3. An interval.
4. A chord.
5. G♯, C♯, B♯.
6. An interval in which two notes have the same pitch.
7. The harp.
8. Beats or beating.

## CHAPTER 2:

1. Diminished 4th (if the letter-names are the same as before) or major 3rd.
2. One interval is the inversion of the other.
3. A minor 9th.
4. There are nine half-steps in a diminished 7th, and two half-steps in a diminished 3rd.
5. Diminished 5th, augmented 4th, tritone.
6. The 3rd is a modal step of the scale. Modal steps occur in two principal forms – major and minor. The 5th is a tonal step. Tonal steps occur in one primary form – perfect.
7. A major interval always contains one more half-step than the minor interval with the same number of scale steps.
8. F♯, E, E♯ (not F; F is an augmented 4th below B, not a diminished 5th).
9. Minor 6th, major 7th, diminished 5th.
10. An augmented octave.

## CHAPTER 3:

1. An augmented triad.
2. E major: E, G♯, B; B minor: B, D, F♯; B♭ major: B♭, D, F; A augmented: A, C♯, E♯ (not F); E♭ major: E♭, G, B♭; F♯ minor: F♯, A, C♯; G diminished: G, B♭, D♭; F diminished: F, A♭, C♭ (not B); D major: D, F♯, A.

3. Dm: D, F, A; F: F, A, C; Adim: A, C, E♭; B: B, D♯, F♯; A♭aug: A♭, C, E; Cm: C, E♭, G; B♭: B♭, D, F; D♭: D♭, F, A♭; Gaug: G, B, D♯; E♭m: E♭, G♭, B♭.

4. First inversion.

5. There are four augmented triads.

6. A.

7. First inversion.

8. A minor triad.

9. The root and 5th are doubled more often, the 3rd less often.

10. An open voicing contains gaps into which notes belonging to the chord could be inserted. In a closed voicing, the notes of the chord are as close together as possible.

## CHAPTER 4:

1. The changes are the chords used in a song, as assigned to the measures of the song. Harmonic rhythm is the rhythm with which the chords in a progression change. The relative minor of a major key is the minor key whose tonic is a minor 3rd below the tonic of the major key; both keys use the same key signature. A deceptive cadence is a chord progression in which a dominant (V) chord moves to some other chord than the tonic (I). A riff is a short chord progression (or a bass or melodic line) that is repeated.

2. C♯ minor, C major, C♯ diminished (or C♯ minor, if the 6th step of the B minor scale is raised).

3. The tonic.

4. The V chord in minor is usually altered so that it has a major 3rd (the leading tone of the scale). The IV chord is occasionally altered so that it also has a major 3rd. Note that if the 6th and 7th steps of the minor scale are raised in this fashion, all of the diatonic triads except I are altered: II changes from diminished to minor and III from major to augmented because their 5ths are raised, while VI and VII change from major to diminished because their roots are raised. Because the 7th step of the scale is raised more often than the 6th, the triads that are most often affected (at least potentially) are III, V, and VII.

5. The progression in Figure 4-15 is I-II-V-VI-IV-I-II-V-I. The first Dm chord is in first inversion, and so is the C chord in bar 2.

6. The VII triad is used less often than the other diatonic triads, because it's diminished.

# CHAPTER 5:

1. Augmented-major 7th, major 7th, dominant 7th, minor-major 7th, minor 7th, half-diminished 7th, diminished 7th (shown in this order in the figure).

2. Minor 7 flat 5 (m7♭5).
3. Three.
4. The tonic.
5. Cm7: C, E♭, G, B♭; Emaj7: Amaj7: A, C♯, E, G♯; F7: F, A, C, E♭.
6. A triad.
7. The 5th can be most easily omitted.
8. An E7 chord.
9. The lowest notes would be C and D♯.
10. None of them.
11. F♯ diminished; G♭ augmented; A major.
12. F. The chord would be a Gm7 in third inversion.

# CHAPTER 6:

1. A chord consisting of stacked 2nds is a cluster-chord.
2. Bitonalism.
3. It's a suspended 4th (sus4).
4. Root, 3rd, 5th, 7th, and 9th. The question does not give enough information to say whether any of the notes above the root is major, minor, augmented, or diminished.
5. Because the note a 15th above the root of a chord is another root.
6. Dmaj9: D, F♯, A, C♯, E; B♭7♯11: B♭, D, F, A♭, C, E; Em11: E, G, B, D, F♯, A; F7♭9♯9: F, A, C, E♭, G♭, G♯ (the last note can optionally be spelled A♭).
7. A flat 5th is the same as a sharp 11th. An augmented 13th would be the same note as the minor 7th.
8. Cm7. A 6 chord sounds sweet.

# CHAPTER 7:

1. Ionian (C), Dorian (D), Phrygian (E), Lydian (F), Mixolydian (G), Aeolian (A), Locrian (B).
2. Lydian has a raised 4th step. Phrygian and Locrian have a lowered 2nd step.

3. An anticipation.
4. A passing tone.
5. W-H-W-W-W-W-H.
6. The harmonic minor.
7. F Dorian (or possibly F Aeolian).
8. Two whole-tone scales and three diminished scales.
9. Five tones.
10. A blue note is a note of the scale that is being played flat or sharp, and not necessarily by an equal-tempered half-step. Except when played on a keyboard, blue notes are "in the cracks" between equal-tempered pitches.
11. D minor pentatonic (which is the same as F major pentatonic).
12. The perfect 4th or perfect 5th.

## CHAPTER 8:

1. A turnaround.
2. Three.
3. A chorus is one iteration of — in other words, once through — the entire chord progression (often, though not necessarily, 32 bars in length).
4. A tag is a portion of a song or arrangement, usually brief, that is played at the end of a chorus or the end of the entire performance of the song.
5. Modulation.
6. A pedal (or pedal tone).
7. Contrary motion.
8. E♭. G.

# INDEX

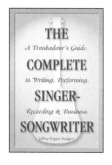
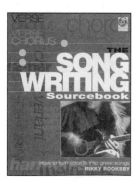